BOSE OR GANDHI

Who Got India Her Freedom?

Maj Gen (Dr) **G D Bakshi** SM, VSM (Retd)

KW Publishers Pvt Ltd
New Delhi

Fifth reprint with a new Postscript, September 2019
Sixth reprint, January 2020

ISBN 978-93-87324-67-1 Paperback
eISBN 978-93-87324-68-8 ebook

Published in India by Kalpana Shukla

KW Publishers Pvt Ltd
4676/21, First Floor,
Ansari Road,
Daryaganj,
New Delhi 110002
P: +91 11 43528107
E: kw@kwpub.com
W: www.kwpub.com

Printed and bound in India.

Contents

Dedicated
To Netaji Subhash Chandra Bose
and
All Ranks past and present
of
The Indian National Army
Whose enormous sacrifices made us free.
We chose however
to carve not a line
and raise not a stone,
in their sacred memory.

Acknowledgements

The author wishes to specifically place on record his immense gratitude and debt to Dr Kalyan Kumar Dey, author of the excellent book "Netaji Subhas: The Liberator of Indian Subcontinant", for permission to quote extensively from his research work. The author is also deeply indepted to Dr Mithi Mukherji of the University of Colorado for permission to quote extensively from her most insightful book "India in the Shadow of Empire: A Legal and Political History 1914-1950". I also wish to record my gratitude to my wife Suneeta for typing and editing this work and to my children, Aditya and Purnima for their constructive suggestions and insights. I thank my grand children Samar and Anahita for letting me use the computer while they sportingly played their computer games on the lap top. Lastly, I am indebted to Ms Kalpana Shukla and Jose Mathew of KW Publishers for their excellent editorial and production support and encouragement without which this book would not have been possible.

Maj Gen (Dr) **GD Bakshi**, SM, VSM (Retd)

Key British Decision Makers 1945-47

Lord Clement Attlee
Prime Minister

Pethick-Lawrence
Secretary of
State for India

Field Marshal
Archibald Percival
Wavell Viceroy

Field Marshal
Sir Claude Auchinleck
Commander in Chief
in India

Prologue
Defining The Civilisational Context of The Debate

The Destruction of the Idea of India

A historical overview of the trajectory of the civilisational nation state of India , is very essential to put this book and its very challenging theme—of *who got India her freedom and how*—in proper perspective. *No other nation in the world has faced such a concerted assault upon its identity and sense of nationhood and self, than India.* Nation states are entities that have a temporal existence over vast stretches of space and across centuries in time. The problem with India was the comprehensive destruction it faced via a series of bloody invasions. These had originally started in the seventh century AD itself, with the invasions of the Hindu kingdoms of Afghanistan and Sindh by the Arab armies. The little-known fact of history is that, for three centuries, the Hindu Kingdoms of Kabul and Zabul had held off the Arab Invaders. In fact the all-conquering Arab Armies suffered their first major defeat in Hindu Afghanistan (and have since been talking of the unfinished Gazwa-e-Hind—the final battle for the conquest of India, which will happen at the end of time). The Arab invasion of Sindh was halted by the Gujjar-Pratiharas on the borders of Rajasthan, contained and prevented from advancing any further for the next two centuries.

The ramparts of India finally fell when the Afghan Hindus were converted to Islam and mounted a series of raids on North India to loot its fabulous wealth. These started in the tenth century AD as bloody raids for plunder, gold and women and once the fact of India's lack of unity, pacific nature and military weakness were thoroughly exposed, came the wars of conquest. From the thirteenth century onwards India faced a series of invasions where the marauders who came to loot and rape, stayed back to rule. *So vast was the temporal extent of India, however, that no single invader, not the Mughals nor the British could conquer it in its entirety.* Thus enclaves of the Indian culture survived and thrived in the southern parts of India for centuries even as the Northern Parts were being overrun by the Armies of Islam. Thus even while North India fell to Afghans, Mongols, Mughals and, much later, Persian invaders, the Cholas of the South were making naval forays and spreading Indian culture and values and its arts and architecture to large parts of South East Asia.

Thus it was the sheer size and extent and the very depth of the temporal existence of the Indian civilisation in time and space, that prevented this civilisation from being wholly overrun and destroyed. It was simply its great depth in space and time that saved the Indian civilisation from being wiped out. *Few historians, however, highlight the remarkable fact that for over 400 years, i.e., from the thirteenth to the seventeenth century, India was ruled by Muslim_invaders. Yet over 80% of the Indian population remained Hindu.* This is a stark contrast with the equally ancient and flourishing civilizations of Egypt, Mesopotamia, Central Asia and Iran which were converted en masse to Islam. There is not a trace of their original indigenous culture left today. The Parsis in India are all that remains of the flourishing Persian civilisation of Iran. How did this miracle happen? India *proved to be a weak state but was a strong society. Thus once the Hindu states in India were militarily overrun, Indian society deliberately splintered itself into a plethora of Jatis, varna and caste groups which kept their flocks together by the severe threat of social boycott and excommunication.* They threatened all who converted with excommunication—via stopping all ties of consanguineous eating or marriage (*Roti, beti ka rishta,* ties of eating together and giving daughters in marriage). These were desperate, last- ditch measures to preserve gene pool purity. Thus a plethora of castes and *Gotra* groups arose in India which tightly shepherded their local flocks via largely localised jat biradaries or clan groupings. The Hindu political states were destroyed by invading Muslim armies but the natives held themselves together in the face of untold persecution by banding together in Jat and Biradari clusters at the local level. *This prevented comprehensive penetration of Hindu Society by the proselytising attempts of Islam. Despite conquest by military force, Islam was not able to convert the entire mass of the huge Hindu population to Islam. The sheer contrast with what happened in Egypt, Mesopotamia, Central Asia and Iran could not be more marked.*

Unfortunately today the caste system is an anachronism in India. The simple fact is that India is now a full fledged state and we don't need to fall back anymore on our last line of defence—the caste and jati groups. In fact today these are hindering the formation of a strong and cohesive nation state in India. As societies industrialise and urbanise, caste becomes a meaningless anachronism. It should have withered out completely by now but our pygmy politicians have kept it alive because they have failed to generate any other national issues except Caste and Jati-based mobilisation. This is now threatening the very unity of India and could once again imperil the existence of the nation state in India.

Britain's Psychological Enslavement

The British came to India in the sixteenth century when the Mughal Empire was in its heyday with Jehangir and Shah Jahan ruling in great opulence and splendour. The Mughal Empire was then generating some 40% of the world's GDP. The British came as petty traders to sell silver and buy back Indian spices and hand woven cloth. Then came Aurangzeb who undid the secular-liberal consensus on the basis of which Akbar had founded the Mughal Empire. He reintroduced the hated Jaziya tax and started mindless wars of conquest in South India to further expand the Mughal Empire. The temporal spread in spatial terms, was simply too much to control. The Mughal Empire suffered an economic collapse because of Aurangzeb's mindless wars. Afghanistan slipped from the grasp of the Mughal empire but what was even more telling was the massive revolts of the Hindus against the tyrannical repression of Aurangzeb. These had gravely threatened the Hindu identity per se and, faced with genocide, they revolted. These revolts were led by Shivaji Maratha in the South and the Sikhs of Guru Gobind Singh in the North. In the East an Assamese General called Lachit Burpukhan decisively checked any Mughal advance to the East and saved Assam and the North East from falling prey to the Mughals. Within one century, the mighty Mughal Empire, which once encompassed the whole of South Asia, had been torn apart. Thus it was not the British who saved the Hindus from Muslim persecution in India but rather it were the Hindu revolts that had comprehensively destroyed the Mughal empire, well before the British began their wars of conquest.

The Human Terrain in India at the Time of the British Conquest

The British studied the human terrain in India with great thoroughness. They were good anthropologists and strategists. They fully exploited the chaos caused by the destruction of the well-established Mughal empire. No single power had arisen in India which could truly as yet, step into the shoes of the Mughal empire. The Marathas had conquered large parts of Central India, the peninsular and even Western India. The Sikhs conquered most of North-Western India up to the borders of Afghanistan and even conquered parts of Afghanistan on the Southern banks of the Indus (NWFP, and FATA). Dogra Generals of the Sikh Empire of Maharaja Ranjit Singh (Generals Gulab Singh and Zorawar Singh) conquered Ladakh, Baltistan and then invaded Tibet itself. What we were witnessing was a Hindu military renaissance.

Nativisation

Into this warring cauldron of states in India, stepped the East India Company and other European powers. In true Machiavellian style they played one power off against the other—the Marathas against the Nizam; the Sikhs against the Purbayias (Easterners) of modern-day UP, Bihar and Bengal and so on. The British success lay in nativisation. They recruited local Indian sepoys, trained them on European lines to create first-rate infantry units that could fire in disciplined rhythm that could defeat any Mughal-style cavalry charge. The British artillery was the best in South Asia then. The well-drilled British native infantry could then outfight all Mughal style cavalries in India. It was amongst the best paid and administered of the military units in India. By a combination of sheer intrigue, and Intelligence-based operations, of playing one off against the other, the British slowly but steadily captured large swathes of territory in India. The Mughal empire had been destroyed but no single Hindu state had emerged in India to form a unified political state that could now do away with the plethora of castes and communities that had been created as a last ditch line of defence to safeguard Hindu society against Muslim proselytisation—whether by force or preaching. The British played one ethnicity based state in India against the other. They fought successive wars against the Marathas, the Nizam and Tipu Sultan and then the Sikhs. They used the Poorbiyas to defeat the Sikhs and then, when the Poorbiyas revolted en masse against their British masters for their proselytising zeal, they used the Sikhs and the hill tribes against them to brutally suppress the revolt of 1857.

Post-1857 British Consolidation

Thus Sir John Seeley wrote: *"The mutiny was in great measure put down by turning the races of India against each other. So long as this can be done, the government of India from England is possible. But, if this were to change and should the population be moulded into a single nationality, we would have to leave."* The 1857 Revolt had left the British truly shaken. *It cured them of their proselytising zeal. They realised that any attempts to convert by force or fraud threatened to unleash wars of Identity per se* in India. What really perturbed them however was the fact that all the diverse races, castes and creeds of India had united in an attempt to throw the hated British out. The British were really the non-self, that was refusing to merge into the Indian civilisation, and in fact, the British were threatening deep-rooted Indian identities based on religion. This threat to Hindu and Muslim identities based on greased cartridges, almost blew the empire apart. *The greatest British concern after the 1857 uprising therefore was how to ensure that the disparate and fragmented Indian population remained divided and never, ever came together again to stage such a massive and widespread rebellion.* It was the very British non-self, their foreignness, and refusal to Indianise in any manner that generated large-scale opposition and rebellion. It is noteworthy that the Mughals had Indianised themselves to a large extent by adopting Indian cultural mores and even learnt to appreciate Indian classical dance and music. Dara Shikoh had the Upanishads translated into Persian and before him Akbar had tried to formulate a new synthesis of faiths in India by his Deen-e-Elahi. The very arrogant Foreignness of British rule in India, their racial claims of superiority, really helped to initiate the rise and revival on the national self in India. The whole of India had united against the very Foreignness of British rule. The Indian self had begun to crystallise only in relation to a British non-self.

The British Raj now did away with the rule of the British East India Company and the Crown in England took direct charge. Its primary problems in reasserting its rule in India was twofold:

- **Foreignness.** The primary concern was how to overcome the very foreignness of its rule which automatically presented a hostile non-self which in turn would by itself promote national unity and a crystallisation of the Indian sense of self.
- **Fracturing Sources of Indian Unity.** The second was to identify and destroy all sense of Indian unity and cultural identity. Thus Dr. Mithi Mukherjee writes: *If the British Empire had to survive in India ... it had to destroy and*

> *dismantle all sources of Indian unity and identity—cultural, political and historical; and render the very idea of India as meaningless.... Torn by internal conflict, it was claimed that India was in desperate need of a neutral and impartial power at the helm of the state to secure justice and order (or justice as order). Given that Indian society was deeply divided into communities in conflict with each other, only an alien, foreign power could be trusted to be neutral and impartial."*

Thus the British answer to its problems of mitigating the foreignness of its rule was not the Mughal idea of assimilation of Indian culture and ethos to blend and not exacerbate identities that would grate, but to blend rather seamlessly. The British however devised the ideology of imperial justice. They claimed India was no nation. it was just a squabbling and vicious mosaic of multiple identities forever at war with itself. India was a land of multiple identities. After the political and military destruction of the Hindu states in India from the thirteenth century onwards, in a last ditch and desperate attempt to safeguard its identity, the Hindu states had fragmented themselves into a plethora of multiple and highly localised Jat-Biradaries of caste and sub-caste groups. This was to prevent proselytisation by Islam. When Aurangzeb threatened the residual Hindu identity by conversion by violence, there was an explosion. The Maratha and Sikh Revolts thereafter destroyed the Mughal empire. However, no one single successor state was able to crystallise in India. Had this happened, *the re-emergence of a Hindu political state would have demanded an end to the caste and Jati-based local identities that had emerged as last line of defence during Mughal rule.* That however did not happen and in the meantime the British brought the coal-based industrial revolution to India and conquered most of it. Their rather aggressive initial attempts at proselytisation backfired in the revolt of 1857. Thereafter their ardour for Christian proselytization cooled distinctly. Attempts at religious conversion were now largely confined to remote tribal areas (where they were rather successful—especially in the North East).

Exacerbating Caste Faultlines

However attempts to exploit every possible faultline in India were intensified greatly. One of the most effective faultlines they found was caste. The British went out of the way to deepen and intensify every Caste and Jati faultline in India. As Prof. Mtihi Mukherjee writes: *"The British ratified caste by means of various colonial instruments such as district manuals, Gazettes, imperial surveys and finally the Census of 1872; and made Varna, the hierarchical ordering of castes into four groups as the central idea behind classification of Indian society."* She adds, *"The census administration was driven by the ideological need to naturalise the absence of national unity and then institutionalise it by integrating it into routine administrative decisions and policies."*

Sir John Risley was the author of the first caste-based census in India in 1872. He rubbed it in further by saying, "Indians do not have the capacity to develop an idea of nationality, let alone rule themselves." He ascribed it primarily to the institution of caste. "*So long as a regime of castes persists, it is difficult to see how the sentiments of unity and solidarity can penetrate and inspire all classes of the community.*" This polarisation of caste was begun as the pursuit of social justice and was the primary colonial mechanism for splintering and dividing the Indian population, of which the Hindus then constituted well over 80%. Many reform movements In india understood this great weakness and disunity that was inherent in the Hindu caste system. Thus the Sikh Gurus in Punjab made the first attempt to downplay caste faultlines and do away with caste all together. In the bargain a new religion was created and the British tried energetically to prod the Sikhs into becoming a separate religion by way of promoting only *Kesh Dharies* and not *Nam Dharies* to be recruited for the Army. The next was Maharishi Dayananda, founder of the Arya Samaj who found caste to be fatal to Hindu unity as a people and worked energetically to homogenise Hindu society.

Religion and Community Based Electorates

The British turned the concept of divide and rule into a highly sophisticated art form. Thus, after caste, they now decided to deepen Indian religion-based faultlines by providing community-based electorates. Thus the Muslims were the first to get a separate electorate, followed by the Christians and Sikhs and then it was given to the Scheduled Castes and Tribes. The British made energetic attempts to hive off the Dalits (SC and ST) from the Hindu mainstream even as they had successfully segregated the Sikhs from the Hindu fold. At the time of 1857 the British had been alarmed by Muslim pirs and potentates who, to their minds, had tried to restore Mughal rule in India. It is true that the sepoys had forced the luckless Bahadur Shah to resume the mantle of Mughal Emperor. For a time, therefore, the Raj seemed to favour the Hindus against the Muslims but by the onset of the twentieth century, things had come full circle. Now the Hindus were most active against the British in the form of the revolutionaries and the more pacific Congress. The British now most aggressively championed every Muslim cause and manoeuvred to so deepen the Hindu-Muslim Faultline that it finally resulted in the tragic Partition of India. The British had most cleverly played upon and fanned the Muslim fears of being subsumed by a vast Hindu majority.

The Concept of Imperial Justice

This entire gamut of divide and rule policies were designed to permanently deepen and so exacerbate the faultlines in Indian Society that it would reinforce the colonial narrative of Imperial Justice. The basic tenet was an a priori acceptance that India was intrinsically such a hopelessly divided society that it needed Foreign rule to ensure even-handed justice between its perpetually warring castes, creeds, religions and language communities. Only a foreign power could provide such an impartial and fair rule by enforcing the concept of Imperial Justice. Thus the very Foreignness of the British Empire was turned into an inherent advantage and in fact, the very justification for imposing foreign rule in India. Mithi Mukherjee puts it succinctly when she writes: "Torn by internal conflict, it was claimed that *India was in desperate need of a neutral and impartial power at the helm of the state to secure justice and order (or justice as order).* Given that Indian society was deeply divided into communities in conflict with each other, *only an alien, foreign power could be trusted to be neutral and impartial.*" Thus was the ideological basis laid for persistent foreign rule in India that lasted two centuries. The concept of Imperial Justice was specifically created to justify foreign rule in a deeply divided and fractured Indian society. Dr. Mithi Mukherjee writes, "*For India to have any order and unity, the state would have to be exterior to the civil society and nation. It was this intervention of the discourse of Imperial Justice, coupled with state's representation of India as a deeply divided society that tried to turn the exteriority and foreign origin of the colonial state into its greatest strength, rather than a weakness.*"

What Ails Indian Nationalism Today

All the ills that plague nation state formation in India today stem from one basic foundational problem. The British were ultimately forced out of India not by Mahtama Gandhi and Nehru's non-violent freedom struggle but rather starkly by the INA that Bose had formed with Japanese help. He had mounted an invasion of India along with the Japanese armies. Tragically this invasion failed because it had been launched too late—when America had intervened on the side of the Allies and tilted the scales with its huge industrial base. Air superiority had now shifted to the allies and they used it to good effect to counter the highly successful Japanese tactics of infiltration and encirclement. Despite this it was a close fought battle in Imphal-Kohima and the Japanese almost pulled it off. The monsoons destroyed the logistical support of their offensive, forcing them into a costly and painful retreat. After the war the victorious British were in no mood to relent. They in fact decided upon the equivalent of another psychological Jallianwala Bagh by staging the trials of INA Officers at the historic Red Fort—the same iconic Fort where the last Mughal Emperor of India had been tried. *The trial was to be highly publicised to terrorise and overawe the Indian Army Personnel* so that the Ghost of Bose and his INA could be exorcised forever. Bose had been right—the Centre of Gravity of the British Raj had been the steadfast loyalty of the native Indian Sepoy to the Raj. The INA trials were staged to ensure the Sepoy remained so loyal. *It backfired very badly and had the exact opposite effect. The entire country was enraged and riots broke out in all major cities in November 1945*—in the immediate aftermath of the trials. The Colonial dispensation was shaken to the roots by the fury and intensity of these riots. What was worse was the ominous impact it had on the loyalty of the native troops. The whole country now saw the INA as true patriots and the Indian sepoys realised they had clearly been on the wrong side in the war.

The Viceroy and the Commander-in-Chief in New Delhi, Fd Mshls Wavell and Auchinleck, realised the intensity of the emotions unleashed and the gravity of the situation. So did the Governors in the provinces. British troops were drained and spent. They were desperately tired after six years of war and truly homesick. They were being sent back. There were 2.5 million combat hardened Indian soldiers in India then, who were being demobilised. Should they have revolted against the empire, the handful of British troops would have been in no position to quell such an uprising. There was in fact panic in Lutyens, New Delhi and desperate contingency plans were drawn up to face such an emergency and evacuate some 90,000 Europeans and their families. Initially the Raj Imperialists in London felt their functionaries In Delhi had lost their nerves, and they were yet in no mood to throw in the towel. Then in February 1946 came the widespread mutiny in the Royal Indian Navy. Some 20,000 sailors on 79 Ships and many shore establishments took part. This was the last straw that broke the camel's back in London. They realised with a shock that Wavell and Auchinleck were old India hands and were not being alarmist. What they had warned against had indeed come to pass. Just one day after the Naval mutiny the British leadership in London threw in the towel. Pethick-Lawrence announced that he and Stafford Cripps and A. V. Alexander would go to India for final negotiations.

That was the end of the Raj. So the historical fact is that India got its freedom not because of the long-winded and largely ineffectual Non-violent Movement but by the actual and implied violence of Bose and his INA. There lies the tragedy. *Power, however, did not go to Bose or the trenchantly anti-British INA but to the people who had virtually collaborated with the British.* While others fought and laid down their lives, these Congress leaders waited patiently on the sidelines to grab the fruits of power. This was a largely venal and self-serving elite who had not been baptised by fire or tested in an armed struggle. Forgotten in this pacific hoopla and self- congratulations were some 26,000 INA soldiers who had laid down their lives to free the country. The amazing fact is that, of the 60,000 INA, some 26,000 had laid down their lives. It was an enormous scale of suffering and sacrifice to lose 43% of the entire force. Yet The court Historians have the temerity to call the Indian Freedom Struggle an entitrely Non-violent affair. However, the 14,000 or so INA Boys who were repatriated from POW Camps were not taken back into the Indian Army. In fact they were treated as traitors and denied their wartime pensions. The pity is even 70 years after Independence, they still are. They are not allowed to take part in the Republic Day parade—even as veterans. What has been rejected is the very basic Nationalist ideology of Bose and the INA.

Bose vs Nehru—Serious Ideological Differences

So is this a lament for Bose and his INA? No, it is rather a lament for the nation state in India which is still tied to the apron strings of the Raj and has adopted its narratives and kept intact its basic colonial constructs. The Indian Constitution is basically a reprint of the British India Act of 1935 and wholly retains the colonial ethos via its replacement of "Imperial Justice" by "Social Justice." *Its basic premise is that India is not, and never was, a nation state before 1947.* It is a mosaic of constantly warring and squabbling castes, communities and creeds. *The main task of the Indian Government, à la the colonial regime, is to arbitrate between these competing castes and creeds in a just and fair manner,* hence the overriding emphasis on the principle of Social Justice in the Indian Constitution. It has deftly replaced the colonial concept of Imperial Justice. The former bootlickers of the British have ensured that no attempt should ever be made to homogenise the Indian population and all the cultural differences must be maintained in their purity .The emphasis is less on unity and far more on preserving diversity. No effort has been wasted in creating a Pan-Indian Identity. The post-independence politics are purely based on the tribalism of caste Arithmetic. *No post-colonial dispensation in India (not the Congress nor the BJP or any other party) has mustered the courage to go beyond caste.* Caste, as a divisive factor, has only been enhanced and deepened by a host of petty and self-serving politicians who spread the ambit of affirmative action by including more and more caste groups into the ambit of reservations. Today 50% of the Indian population comes under the ambit of caste-based reservations and the clamour is only to widen it further. The Marathas, the Jats, the Gujjars are all up in arms today. *The tragic fact is that the minority of "Indians " in India is in serious decline. The idea of India is under concerted assault by the coalition of castes and creeds. A Govt led by Bose would have seriously contested this colonial narrative and made a concerted attempt to alter the very nature and ethos of the nation state in India.* It would have been reinvented in a radical new form. There was a need for a basic Paradigm Shift from the colonial narrative based on an India of competing castes and creeds. *Had a genuinely nationalist state taken charge in India after independence, its first priority would have been to deepen the idea of India by downplaying strongly the plethora of caste and creed identities and homogenising the state.* Bose was a Realist. He wanted to obliterate all faultlines of caste and creed. He had done so in the INA by doing away with the Jati and Ethnicity based Regiments of the British Indian army and homogenised all INA units on the all-India all-class model.

Militarising the Indian State vs Demilitarisation

Secondly, *the state in India had to be re-consolidated and strengthened as a means of protecting its citizens from foreign invasions and internal disorder. Bose wanted India to have an army of some 3 million men.* Like Mao of China, he was a militarist. The Nehruvian state turned pacific with a vengeance. It flatly said it needed no armed forces. This is the critical factor—*Bose wanted to Industrialise india and make it a major Military power, a significant force on the global arena. Nehru actually wanted to disband the Indian army.* There was no need for an Indian army for a pacific, non-violent country like India, he felt. The police would suffice to protect this state! Fortunately, Patel a realist, prevented Nehru from having his way. India has since had to fight five wars and still faces grave internal and external challenges. In true Gandhian fashion today, the Indian state refuses to fight Pakistan or China, even when its basic national interests are challenged. Given the tragic history of 10 centuries of invasions, this is a recipe for civilisational disaster. We lost those wars and were enslaved—precisely because of our lack of interest in matters military. We will have to revive the legacy of Bose to militarise ourselves, to defend ourselves and not subordinate the state in India to some universalist human rights principles, which the powerful states of the world (like America, China and Russia) today violate with impunity whenever it suits their core national interests. *The Indian civilisational state had been subjected to virtually 10 centuries of defeat and humiliation. Just one century of such humiliation had prompted China to Militarise and reinvent itself in a far more homogeneous and coherent form.* Today China is the second largest military and economic power in the world and well on its way to perhaps becoming the most powerful state on the planet—a Superpower in the true sense of the word. India is still mired in the colonial desideratum of divisive caste and creed loyalties that are threatening to tear apart the very fabric of its unity. The colonial destruction of the very Idea of India, remains complete and total. We have not been able to rebuild what the British had so thoroughly destroyed. *What we needed was a strong state to protect the people of India from external invasions and internal disorders.* Today we have a nation state that claims to be committed to the defence of the idea of India but has hesitated to act in a decisive manner against any of our external and internal enemies. It continues to trumpet the pacific and war-avoiding legacy of Mahatma Gandhi and not the strong Nationalism of Bose and his emphasis not on the soft power of ahimsa but on the hard power of military force. Bose was a realist. *Today we have chosen to stay mired in a dream world of non-violence and ahimsa, when the world around us grows more violent by the day. For a country that has been invaded, subjugated, destroyed, looted and raped for 10 centuries , non-violence is a manifestation of abject cowardice masquerading as high principle.* Let us not forget Mahatma Gandhi himself had decried such cowardice.

What we needed was a strong state in India that would militarise and arm itself to defend its citizens. It chose instead to defend the principles of non-violence and pacifism. A set of very hostile neighbours quickly disabused the Indian nation state of its notions of Non-violence and Ahimsa. A State that cannot defend itself, tragically dies unsung and unwept in today's Darwinian era of the strong eat the weak and devil take the hindmost. We may not militarise in the Germanic sense, but the very least we need is to defend ourselves with vigour and ensure that all such wars to defend India do not take place on Indian soil à la Panipat all over again. Take a look at J&K—that is precisely what is happening there today. We are fighting in a wholly defensive, reactive format confined entirely to Consequence-Management on our own side of the Border. Bose would have made India militarily very strong. He was the only leader of the Freedom Struggle who understood the military idiom. The other political rulers of India know very little of military matters and have not bothered to learn. They have used civil and police bureaucracies to muzzle the military in India and marginalise it from all decision making. We have repeatedly paid the price for it but we simply refuse to learn.

Doing Away with the Legacy of Caste and Creed

As I have said, the Colonial state in India started with the a priori assumption that there was no nation called India—that India had never been a nation state. How then were China and Japan chracterised as nation states? They were much more homogeneous societies. India, you had to accept, was a cauldron of castes and creeds but the British construct was that it needed Foreign Rule for good governance. *If caste and creed were to be used as justifications for Foreign rule and colonisation, then the first task of any new born nation state in India was to do away with caste and creed all together.* Instead, what did the newborn state and its power grasping politicians do? *They deepened the idea of Caste as basic identity by now adding economic tags on the caste identity. Affirmative action was needed primarily for the SC and ST—especially the latter who were most deprived and backward.* A series of self-serving and petty politicians like V. P. Singh, added some 50% of the Indian population into the reserved category. This tends to drive all talent and merit-based selection criterion into the dustbin. *It has created a Communism of Caste, a stifling mediocrity that serves to drive out all our talent to Foreign lands. Even Ambedkar, the framer of our Constitution, had wanted caste-based reservations to be a temporary phenomena.* The present breed of Politicians in India, Congress or otherwise, want to freeze caste-based reservations in perpetuity, for the next 10,000 years perhaps. One fails to understand the Leftist discourse and diatribes against Brahmins and so-called upper class elites. If Muslims ruled India from virtually the tenth century onwards, how were the Brahmins and upper-class people the real power wielders and brokers? They were the most persecuted of the lot in Muslim-ruled states and have been out of power as social groups virtually for the past 800 years. During the British rule, however, they mastered and excelled in the new system of education and in a merit-based mileu, came back to the fore. I am not at all trying to justify the caricatures of the caste system like untouchability, etc., which were abominable practices, and we have taken energetic action to eradicate them. As an independent nation state, however, *we cannot afford to emphasise caste and clan-based identities which make the society regress to tribalism.* That was a desperate, last-ditch mechanism for defence against Proselytisation by the invading Muslim Armies. They came as a defence mechanism when the Hindu states in India failed politically and militarily. They were destroyed and in no position to defend their people. So the people had to fall back on local caste and Jati clusters and Khap panchayats. The Indian nation state has now been in existence for the last 70 years. It is the duty of the nation state to protect its people and their way of life. What have we done to eradicate the sub-identities of caste and creed which now threaten the nation state and militate against a pan-Indian identity. A nation state has to homogenise to an extent and bring equality of opportunity to all its citizens. *Any sensible state will promote merit and not ensure it is driven out to other countries. That is the surest way to ensure a civilisational disaster. So far our educated elite were eagerly lapped up by other states—notably America and Europe. With protectionism on the rise this is not likely, not any longer.* We have a huge youth bulge today and an alarming shortage of jobs. In such a mileu we have unruly agitations for more and more caste-based reservations. The Jats, the Marathas, the Gujjars, the Patels etc., are all clamouring for reservations on the plea of backwardness. What kind of anomaly do we wish to create? A state based on 80 or 90 per cent reservations? What does that do to the hapless 20% that will be left out of this reservation empire? Presumably for ever. As a civilisation we have actualised Communism to its ultimate degree. We have succeeded in creating a Communism of Caste. It is a most inefficient form of Government which has been uprooted from Russia, China and all East European states. Even China has transformed its economy by liberalising trade and turning capitalist with a vengeance. Our politicians still wish to thrive on the Colonial model of divide and rule based on vote banks and the arithmetic of caste. The sole issue in our elections is caste. *It is a pathetic failure of our colonial era elite to outgrow that system.* Nation building is not the prime concern of these political pygmies. Grabbing and retaining power by any means—fair or foul, is.

Economic Criterion for Affirmative Action

This is the era of Information Technology. Today India has created a miracle with the Aadhaar Card. Let us not use it merely for the state to spy on its citizens and create an Orwellian society. Aadhaar cards are better used to target subsidies to weaker sections of society. Now *with the bulk of the population on the Aadhaar card map, is it not time to switch to an Economic criterion based system of affirmative action? The state should target such economic affirmative action to those who are genuinely economically deprived—those who are genuinely below the poverty line. It should be the state's prime endeavour to bring up these genuinely economically deprived Indians—regardless of caste, creed, gender, religion or language.* They are Poor Indians and must be correctly identified via the agency of Aadhaar cards and helped in a targeted fashion. *This will automatically help the SC and ST category the most. They are genuinely poor and deserve help.* It will weed out of this pernicious Affirmative Action regime, all those who claim it on the sole basis of caste and creed and manufactured narratives of historical deprivation and marginalisation.

That is why the debate about Nation state formation in post-colonial India is so very important. How actually did we become free? What were the true origins and causative factors for a post- colonial state to emerge in India? *The question of who got us our freedom and how would determine the kind of state we have become and lay down our future trajectories of change* or of freezing the status quo in perpetuity. The main contention of this book is that, in actual fact, it was Bose and his INA that truly drove out the British in 1947. Left to non-violence alone, freedom would have come to us in India somewhere in the 1980s or 1990s, just as it had come to South Africa only in April 1994 because it had relied on non-violence alone. The tragedy was that Bose and his INA did not take charge of a free India. They liberated it but were edged out by a self-serving Congress elite that were quite wedded to the colonial past. The British actually handed over power to an Anglophile band of quislings and collaborators of the Raj who loyally continued to keep India mired in its colonial past. They started with the a priori British assumption that India was not a nation but a competing cauldron of Castes and Creeds. The Government of India's sole function was to adjudicate between these caste and community groupings in a just and fair manner. *Hence the Indian Constitution's emphasis on Social Justice, in place of the Colonial concept of Imperial Justice.*

The post-Colonial state in India needed to be militarily strong if it was to outgrow its pacific acceptance and tolerance of abject defeat and foreign rule of centuries. It had to homogenise its society and downplay identities based on caste and creed and emphasise a new pan-India identity. *What the post-colonial state in India needed was a Pardigm shift. What it got instead, was a new elite who kept it wedded to the narratives of the empire.* Between pre- and post-colonial India there was very little difference in basic ideology—Social Justice had replaced Imperial Justice and India is still a competing and squabbling cauldron of caste and creed. All elections are simply based on the arithmetic of caste.

That is why who freed India and why is a seminal and vital debate that will define the basics of our Nationhood.

In the end, I would like to acknowledge my gratitude to two Intellectuals who have provided the Inspiration for large parts of this Book. Dr Kalyan Kumar Dey, whose excellent Monograph (*Netaji Subhash: the True Liberator of India*) has put together all the relevant documentary evidence from the British Transfer of Power archives to prove beyond any reasonable doubt that it was the INA of Bose that actually forced the British to leave. I am most grateful to him, for his permission to quote chapter and verse from his excellent study. The other is Dr. Mithi Mukherjee, of the University of Colorado, whose excellent book, *India in the Shadow of Empire* is perhaps one of the best and most insightful accounts of India's Freedom Struggle available today. It provides an alternative historical narrative of the British Empire in India. I have learnt a great deal from the pioneering works of these two very eminent scholars. This book then seeks to turn the searchlight on our recent past and gain new insights about who we are, how we came into being as a nation state and, most important, where are we headed? In the end, where we are going depends a lot on where we came from.

Why Now? Why this book now, is a simple and logical question. 21 Oct 2018, is the 75th Anniversary of the formation of the Hukumate Azad Hind Govt in exile by Netaji Subhas Bose in Singapore (1943). This was recognised by 12 countries, including the then Soviet Union. Netaji then was the first head of State and Commander in Chief of a Free Indian Govt in exile. Mahatma Gandhi's 150th Birth Anniversary falls on 02 October 2019. It is a most appropriate moment for reflecting upon our recent history and the role of these two great personages in making India free.

1

Who Got Us Our Freedom?

This book is an attempt to rescue the history of our Freedom Struggle from some highly motivated colonial and post-colonial myth making that is patently false and tendentious and that seeks to glorify the "benign" nature of colonial rule in India and keep us forever in its psychological thrall. Most educated Indians tend to view it as an era of emancipation of sorts in our history that served to unite a disparate and ever squabbling people into a cohesive and governable nation state. This was the colonial narrative that had so patently and successfully been imposed on our people. Unfortunately it is still believed by a bulk of our educated population. As long as we do not cast away these psychological crutches, we shall never actualise our full potential as a great civilisational state that is heir to 8,000 years of a glorious history.

This book therefore begins with a seminal and straightforward question—Who really got us our freedom? Was it the INA of Netaji Subhash Chandra Bose and his most credible threat of armed violence or was it Mahatma Gandhi and his methodology of Ahimsa, Non-violence and the mystical mumbo-jumbo of Satyagraha and soul force. What made us free—the Soft power of ahimsa or the Hard power of the INA?

These seminal questions therefore deal primarily with the issue of how India got its freedom. Was it because of the soft power of Ahimsa , non-violence and Satyagraha? Or was the use of force, the hard power employed by Netaji and his INA, instrumental in forcing the Britons to leave? *These are seminal issues about the very how and why of nation state formation in India.* Today, they deserve to be debated and discussed in detail. Where our nation state is headed depends a great deal on where we came from—how we came into being—what were the perspectives that shaped our outlook and institutions then? The simple fact is that *there has been an orchestrated attempt, to falsify our recent history and impart to it a pernicious spin. The entire role of Netaji Subhash Bose and his INA has been more or less effaced from our history books which have been turned into hagiographies for a dynastic leadership.* India is a democracy where we have seen the phenomenon of court historians deliberately distorting history. Bipin Chandra's book on India's Freedom Struggle is a magnum opus that runs into over 600 pages. It devotes just one page and a half to Netaji and the INA. That is simply a quantitative indication of the level and extent of the deliberate distortions in emphasis that are being injected into our post-colonial narratives.

The sad fact is that the empire, even as it was forced to pack its bags and leave, methodically handed over the reins of power to a set of anglophile elite, who were handpicked to keep us in everlasting thrall and beholden to the empire, a part of the British Commonwealth (a useless anachronism in this day and age) and to begin with just a Dominion of the empire and not really an independent nation state. Pakistan, the other dominion carved out of India, had the decency to select one of its own—Mohammad Ali Jinnah as its first Governor General. We indulgently and affectionately appointed Lord Mountbatten—the last British Viceroy as our First Governor General, so overwhelming was the affection of our political elite—especially Nehru—for the British Raj. The pity is that the British had created a set of brown-skinned Englishmen who were cast in their own image and steeped in Macaulay's Colonial education and mindset. These brown-skinned elite would strive very hard to see that we remained loyal to the tenets of the Raj. Britain had conquered India with an army of brown-skinned native sepoys. Its psychological sway and dominance would be perpetuated post- independence by another army of brown-skinned anglophiles and intellectuals who would describe themselves as leftist-liberal intellectuals. These are the new set of native sepoys that carry the burden of empire and ensure that we do not deviate from the history and grand narratives that the British masters had written down for us.

Imperial Justice to Social Justice

How strong and pernicious was the influence of the Raj is borne out by the fact that the entire Constitution of India was more or less a faithful reprint of the British India Act of 1935. Thus the very preamble of the Indian Constitution begins with Social Justice. Why this primacy to social justice? Why not to the principles of Liberty, Fraternity and Equality? Why Social Justice? Because this helped us to deftly replace the Colonial concept of "Imperial Justice," with "Social Justice." This entailed that the new rulers of independent India would forever have to be psychologically extrinsic to the native Indian milieu. Nehru was precisely such a brown-skinned Englishman—he was therefore supposedly beyond the thrall of the plethora of Indian religions, castes and creeds and races and languages. He was not really a Hindu. He was an agnostic. Because of being so very British in orientation, he was above and beyond the morass that was India and could dispense Social Justice between the various castes and creeds without fear or favour. Social Justice had deftly replaced Imperial Justice as the cornerstone of the constitution of the New Republic that had so deeply internalised the colonial narrative. Nehru had been hand-picked by the Raj, which presumably impelled Gandhi to anoint him as the first Prime Minister of India over the administratively far more competent Sardar Patel, who was the choice of the Congress Party per se.

Only the Nehru-Gandhi family was thereafter decreed fit to rule this chaotic mass of disparate people because the Nehru-Gandhi clan were so very British and so "propah!" They alone could dispense social justice instead of the imperial justice that the empire had ruthlessly enforced over the warring, squabbling castes and creeds of India. Thus the very foundation of this Republic was kept confined within the imperial constructs of the Raj. This Weltanschauung sadly reflects in the very Preamble of our constitution.

The British left but they left behind a set of WOGs (Western Oriented Gentlemen) who would forever be beholden to the Raj. These wogs would remain sadly oblivious to the delicious irony that wogs was also the second half of a British term called Golli-wog—a black Doll that was used as a racial term of contempt for the natives who put on airs of being British style gentlemen.

The British left behind a Civil bureaucracy and above all an Intelligence Bureau, many of whose servants retained a residual loyalty to the Raj. The Indian IB had detailed dossiers on many of the political leaders of the new dispensation. So they retained an inordinate amount of influence over the new dispensation. The first head of the IB (B. N. Mullick) became an Edgar Hoover of sorts. He remained the head of the IB for almost 13 years. The Mi-5 left a Liaison Office in New Delhi. Amazingly the Indian IB continued to report to the MI5 in London about the movements of Netaji's kin till almost the end of the decade of the 1960s. Was this with the knowledge and approval of Nehru? Did he know what was going on behind his back, or was it with his express knowledge and approval? These are seminal questions that must be asked and investigated. We must get our own history right. We must outgrow the shackles of psychological slavery and begin to think for ourselves as Indians.

The British left but they left behind a set of lackeys that have kept the nation psychologically enslaved and bound down by the Grand Narratives handed down to us by the empire.

This book therefore begins with a set of seminal and straightforward questions. Who really got us our Azadi? Who really made us free? Was it the INA of Bose and their threat of and actual use of armed violence, or was it the soft power of Mahatma

Gandhi's Satyagraha and non- violence which really got us our freedom?

There is that popular lyric that sums it all up so neatly. It is part of the hagiography that has been so assiduously been built around the legacy of the Nehru-Gandhi dynasty. It says:

"De di hame azaadi bina kharag bina dhaal
Sabarmati ke sant tune kar diya kamaal."

This translates into:

"O saint of Sabarmati You wrought a miracle
You gave us our freedom sans sword and shield."

This lyric is an unabashed insult to the 26,000 martyrs of the INA. The INA had an overall strength of some 60,000. Of these, as per the official INA history, some 26,000 laid down their lives. This amounts to 43% of the Force that was martyred. It is an awe-inspiring scale of casualties and sacrifice and it is an unmitigated insult to all those martyrs to call the Indian Freedom Struggle as entirely peaceful and non-violent. It is a disgraceful lie and patent untruth and you cannot attribute it to a saint who made a fetish of always speaking the truth. A nation that has *Satyamev Jayate* (Truth Alone Triumphs) as its motto cannot subscribe to such a narrative that is at such sharp variance with ground realities and the truth. Why did the Nehru regime spend so much time and energy in crafting a pacific narrative for India? It seemingly harkened back to the times of the Buddha and Ashoka to lay exaggerated claims to a legacy of pacifism and non-violence. Nehru tried to paint himself as another Gautam Buddha come to rid the world of its scourge of war and violence. Why this exaggerated emphasis on a legacy of pacifism that was at obvious variance with much of our historical experience. India's main epics —the Ramayana and the Mahabharata—are all about war and righteous war or just war. India was first unified by military force by the Mauryan Empire of Chandragupta who was guided by the hard realism and realpolitik of Kautilya. This happened in India's period of the warring states when 16 Major States (Maha Janapdas) were constantly at war with one another for supremacy. This was just like in China of the period of warring kingdoms, when 6 major states were at constant war with one another. India's historical strategic culture had emerged in that period of war and violence in the form of Kautilya's Artha Shastra. It was hardly pacific in orientation and urged the ruler to be vijayadishu—a conquerer (who would constantly expand the size and power of his kingdom). Indian pacifism of the later Ashokan period, in fact, cost it dearly as from the tenth century onwards India succumbed to a series of invasions from West Asia and Central Asia which led to a horrific bloodbath amounting to genocide. India was subjugated for 800 years thereafter by foreigners. India had a dire need to militarise and defend itself—not preach non-violence to a very violent world.

The reasons for this policy option were more rooted in Nehru's quest for political legitimacy which was badly threatened by Bose and the violence of the INA which had in reality freed India. The convoluted narrative of an entirely peaceful and non-violent freedom struggle was a deliberately manufactured myth. The British spread it to paint a shining sunset picture of their 200 years of rapacious colonial rule, which they now tried to present in very benevolent and liberal colours. The Nehruvian dispensation did it to present themselves as the true liberators of India who had won her Independence without firing a shot. Twenty-six thousand INA soldiers had been martyred in the Indian struggle for Freedom yet Nehru had the nerve to call it an entirely peaceful struggle. He was fighting with the Ghost of Bose and his INA. But a deeper look suggests something far more serious afoot.

Pacification of Military Cultures

After the Second World War, the Allies made a major effort to pacify the highly militaristic races of Germany and Japan. They had exhibited amazing fighting spirits and intense nationalism. The Americans imposed a pacific culture and constitution on both Germany and Japan. Today these countries are major economic powers, but they remained thoroughly demilitarised and defanged. Not so well known is the fact that another country that the British virtually demilitarised and defanged was India. They simply imposed upon it a Pacific Political leadership with a very exaggerated notion of the efficacy of soft power of Ahimsa (non-violence) as opposed to hard power. The deliberate British design was to leave but instal a pacific Indian leadership that believed in the soft power of Buddhism more than in the hard power of a credible military. The vast military potential of India had become evident to the whole world during World War I and II. India had generated massive armies of 1.3 million and 2.5 million respectively in these two wars. By the time the British left they had reduced the Indian Army from 2.5 million to a pathetic 350,000 which they then divided between the two warring Dominions. How dangerous this was has now been proved by the four wars India had to fight after independence. India's actual security needs have necessitated a new army of 1.3 million men.

Fortunately India was set free from this pacific outlook. The Nehruvian dispensation led India to a disastrous military defeat in the 1962 war with China. This traumatic defeat cured India emphatically of the Nehruvian disease of pacifism. The decade from 1960 to 1970 was the decade of militarisation for India. Just on the heels of the Chinese attack, the Pakistan military decided to inflict a coup de grace on a floundering pacific state. The rump state of Pakistan was one-fifth the size of India. However it had no baggage of abject pacifism. The Americans gifted it huge amounts of cutting edge military equipment and very soon its Army took charge by imposing Martial Law in Pakistan.

As India began to rearm and expand its armed forces in the wake of the 1962 disaster, the self-styled Field Marshal Ayub Khan of Pakistan sensed his last chance to kick in this tottering republic and seize Kashmir. He even dreamt of driving his Patton tanks into New Delhi. A thoroughly chastised Indian political establishment now listened attentively to the advice of its professional military chief. Pakistan's desperate gamble to grab Kashmir by force backfired badly. It led to an escalatory spiral that saw India launch two Corps-sized counteroffensives across the International Border (IB) directed at the key Pakistani cities of Lahore and Sialkot. Pakistan was forced to recoil from Chhamb and fight desperately to save its own existence.

This war was more or less a draw. It was Pakistan's last chance to exploit India's pacifism and defeat India militarily. India's defence modernisation was now put in top gear and by 1971 this process had reached its peak with very generous support from the erstwhile Soviet Union. Resultantly, when Pakistan once again provoked India by pushing out 10 million refugees into India after a general crackdown in East Pakistan, India reacted in a ruthless manner. It launched a massive tri-services campaign to liberate Bangladesh and resettle the refugees. In fourteen action packed days, India won a decisive military victory. It broke Pakistan into two, marched on an enemy capital and enforced regime change. It resulted in the largest mass surrender of forces post the Second World War. Some 93,000 Pakistani troops surrendered in Dacca. India had shaken off the slough of pacifism and won one of its greatest military victories in its entire civilisational history.

This is how a set of wars that were forced upon India impelled it to jettison the post-colonial legacy of pacifism. The fiction created by the empire had sustained this legacy of pacifism. It tried desperately to hide the true causes that had actually compelled the British to leave and tried to sustain the fiction of a non-violent struggle. No one is questioning here the transparent sincerity and dedication of Mahatma Gandhi and what he was able to achieve in terms of making the Indian independence movement a mass-based struggle. He was a saintly figure and truly believed in the need for Ahimsa. No one can ever doubt his transparent sincerity. No less a personage than Subhash Bose himself called Gandhi the "Father of the Nation."

It was just that the Empire found Gandhi's philosophy of pacifism most convenient. Without Gandhi actually knowing it, the British subtly helped to propel him to the forefront of India's Public Awareness. The empire was happy that the Indian struggle for independence was being kept peaceful and non-violent by Gandhi who truly abhorred violence. It is just that the highly manipulative colonial administration subtly tried to prevent a violent overthrow of the Empire in India by directing all protests into non-violent channels that would make it wholly manageable. It painted the Raj in liberal and angelic colours, enabling them to deal with the non-violent agitation with ease. The Raj found non-violence entirely manageable and hence they tacitly encouraged it.

They built up the Gandhi persona into a larger than life figure in South Asia also for the consumption of other colonies in Asia and Africa. They tacitly encouraged his pacific philosophy and ensured it put a lid on all violent protests and wars of Liberation. Sadly, the strategists of the Raj subtly used and exploited the Gandhian philosophy. This form of protest was entirely manageable and they could have sustained themselves in the face of such protests for decades. Had it been left entirely to the non-violent protests and civil disobedience of Gandhi and Nehru, the Raj would have continued and gone on well into the 1980s and perhaps even beyond. This is not a speculation or conjecture. The peaceful Gandhian-style agitation of Nelson Mandela delayed the South African independence till April 1994—almost towards the end of the twentieth century. It was only the very real threat of armed violence and a military threat to the empire that forced the British to pack up their bags and quit India in 1947 itself.

Bose had most astutely understood that the centre of gravity of the Raj was the loyalty of sepoys of the British Indian Army to the colonial regime. *The British success lay in nativisation.* They had used an Army of natives (trained on European lines) to subjugate their own people. When this loyalty unravelled, the British had no option but to leave. *It was Bose therefore who catalysed an early exit of the Raj and dealt it an effective body blow that precipitated its hasty withdrawal.*

The enormous tragedy of it all is that even as the Raj was forced to recede, it broke up India into the antagonistic dominions of India and Pakistan. Even more it left behind a dispensation in New Delhi that was entirely anglophile in outlook and orientation and had in fact collaborated with the Raj in its last days.

Gandhi had surprised the British by launching the Quit India Movement in 1942. He had done it against the advice of Nehru and Azad and, in fact, against the opinion of the entire Congress Working Committee (CWC). The British were fighting a war and were in no mood to indulge the "naked Indian Fakir." They mustered up some five divisions worth of white troops and crushed the Quit India Movement with ridiculous ease. Wartime censorship helped them to banish Gandhi and his freedom struggle from the newspaper headlines. Deprived of the oxygen of publicity, the Quit India Movement collapsed like a pack of cards. Virtually the entire Congress leadership was jailed. When Gandhi went on his customary fast, Churchill decreed that he should be allowed to die unsung. The British now began to rely far more on the highly manipulable Nehru than on Gandhi. Gandhi was finally released in 1944. He was truly broken in spirit. In his press statements he admitted as much.

The Push to Pacifism

I would, however, like to dwell a bit more on the issue of how Britain deliberately pushed the newborn state of India towards Pacifism by imposing on it a leadership that laid exaggerated claims upon a legacy of Non-Violence. Was there a deliberate strategic design to prevent the emergence of a new centre of power in Asia? At the end of World War II India had fielded the largest all-volunteer army in the history of the world. At 2.5 million men what was significant was that this Army had been recruited without any conscription (unlike in Europe, America and the USSR). This army had proved to be professionally robust and reliable. By 1943, British senior commanders had clearly started indicating their preference for Indian divisions and units over British military units that were showing clear signs of war-weariness and fatigue. Indian troops were hardy and Spartan, needed much less logistical support and were tenacious in combat. On both sides in Burma, it was primarily Indian troops who had performed very well in actual combat. *The British were rather keen to disarm India before they went away. They slashed the Indian Army by 85% to leave a rump force.* They left behind a pacific regime that abhorred violence and hated the Armed Forces with a venom and virulence that was surprising. Just like Japan had been pacified and turned into a toothless state after the Second World War. It was forced to adopt pacifism as state policy so that it would never threaten the USA or Europe again; similarly India was defanged before the British left. They demobilised the 2.5 million strong Indian Army into a rump force of some 350,000 men that was then divided between India and Pakistan. Like Mao, Bose had wanted to have an INA that would be 3 million strong and a power to reckon with in Asia and the world. It is noteworthy that the PLA of China had actually reached a peak strength of a staggering 4.2 million men (after the Korean War). Post-World War II the USA had taken care to demilitarise Japan and impose a pacific constitution on it to ensure it would never be a threat again to the USA. The British did better, they simply disbanded India's massive and combat hardened army of 2.5 million men after the War and left behind a set of rulers who had made a fetish out of pacifism (to try and gain legitimacy vis-à-vis Bose, a leader who had fought for India's freedom by violent means and was the key catalyst for their decision to quit India.) To overcome his legacy of violence , they had gone overboard in trying to promote pacifism. Pandit Nehru hated the military and had in fact told the First British Chief of Independent India's Army, that he did not need armed force in India—the police forces would suffice! The look of shock and incredulity on the British General Sir Roy Bucher's face should have been preserved for posterity.

Very fortunately for India, the trauma of partition and the large-scale riots that followed, the Pakistani invasion of J&K and the need to liberate Hyderabad, underlined the inescapable need for military force in a Westphalian state system. Sardar Patel was a strong nationalist leader and a clear-headed realist who understood the need for the use of force in the affairs of state. It was Patel who undid the unholy mosaic of princely states left behind by the British and made India a viable territorial entity in the Westphalian sense. Unfortunately for India, Patel died much too soon after independence.

Post-Patel, the Indian Nation state under Nehru turned with a redoubled vigour to establish a manufactured National Narrative of itself as an exceptional state based not on hard power but a soft power narrative of Ahimsa, moral force and persuasion as opposed to military coercion, compellence and actual use of hard power. India was now part of the Westphalian system of nation states premised upon hard power. India's contrived narrative however said it was a state with a huge difference. It was formed on the basis of soft power of Satyagraha which had driven out the British. Unfortunately, this was not based on empirical historical facts. The British had left because of the military and hard power challenge of the INA and its ability to instigate armed rebellion amongst 2.5 million trained men of the demobilised British Indian Army. If these had rebelled in mass, the battle-weary British were simply in no state to deal with such a massive armed revolt in India. *The Ghost of the INA was capable of initiating precisely such an armed rebellion. That is what made the British quit.* They felt they were perfectly capable of dealing with the non-violent movement. It was only the possibility of large-scale violence by 2.5 million demobilised soldiers that impelled the British not to get bogged down in a military morass and cut their costs and leave, when they did. Let us now analyse this issue in a sequential manner.

2

An Overview of The Freedom Struggle

If the British Empire had to survive in India... it had to destroy and dismantle all sources of Indian unity and identity – cultural, political and historical; and render the very idea of India as meaningless. ... Torn by internal conflict, it was claimed that India was in desperate need of a neutral and impartial power at the helm of the state to secure justice and order (or justice as order). Given that Indian society was deeply divided into communities in conflict with each other, only an alien, foreign power could be trusted to be neutral and impartial.

— Dr Mithi Mukherjee
India in the Shadows of Empire: A Legal and Political History

The mutiny was in great measure put down by turning the races of India against each other. So long as this can be done, the government of India from England is possible. But, if this were to change and should the population be moulded into a single nationality, we would have to leave."

— Sir John Seeley

India has been unified only thrice in its history of over five millenniums. These were the unifications effected by the three great empires in history—the Mauryan Empire, the Mughal Empire and, finally, the British Empire. The present Indian Republic is the successor entity of the British Empire. The reputed German historians, Hermann Kulke and Dietmar Rothermund, have cited the non-revolutionary and smooth transfer of power as enabling the Indian Republic to continue seamlessly, with the institutions fashioned by the British Empire like the Armed Forces, the civil bureaucracy and the police and intelligence services.

The somewhat disconcerting historical fact, however, is that the British did not grant independence to India in 1947. They carried out a *transfer of power* to an Anglophile coterie of lawyers in the Indian National Congress led by Nehru. For the first three years India remained a Dominion of the Empire and became a Republic only in 1950. In hindsight, we can see that its autonomy and autarchy remained subject to *subtle controls and constraints created by an Intelligence service and civil bureaucracy that surprisingly retained elements of loyalty to the Raj which had given them their privileged positions.* Dr. Mithi Mukherjee of the University of Colorado has, in her very original and path-breaking book, *India in the Shadows of Empire: A Legal and Political History (1774-1950)* thrown new light on the Indian Freedom Struggle. Her book links the colonial and post-colonial periods of Indian History into a seamless narrative, and thereby provides a radically new overview on the emergence of India as a modern nation state. To understand the current Indian politics, therefore, we must understand our recent history.

The 1857 Uprising

Aurangzeb had destroyed the secular consensus on which Akbar had built and then taken the Mughal Empire to such great heights. Akbar had monetised the economy on the silver standard and rationalised the taxation regime. He had established matrimonial alliances with the Rajput Princes and co-opted some of them as generals in the Mughal Army. Aurangzeb, however, reintroduced the hated Jazia tax and intensified persecution of the Hindus and Sikhs. He completely unravelled the secular consensus put in place by Akbar (who had called India his Homeland). This led to the revolts of the Sikhs, the

Marathas and the Ahoms in Assam. These revolts had torn apart the Mughal Empire, well before the British established their sway. Into this vacuum, the British East India Company stepped in innocuously. It recruited Indian sepoys, drilled them on European lines and soon created a cost-effective Infantry-based Army that helped it conquer virtually the whole of India, starting from the three coastal bridgeheads of Calcutta, Bombay and Madras. The East India Company was a commercial and mercantile enterprise and intent not upon good governance but the systematic loot of the colonised land and its people. It was also characterised by racial arrogance and deeply ingrained white supremacy attitudes. They destroyed the local crafts and industry to push their mass manufactured products. They cut off the hands of the weavers who used to weave the very fine Muslin cloth of Dacca. Later they forced the locals to cultivate opium for sale to China. Cumulatively, these actions spread great resentment and outrage which finally resulted in the great mutiny of 1857 amongst the sepoy ranks of East India Company's Presidency armies. The spark was provided by the proselytisation efforts and the introduction of greased cartridges said to be dipped in the fat of cows and pigs. This spark soon mutated into a major popular uprising all over North India. Over a period of time, some 80,000 Indian soldiers rebelled. Had they all rebelled together, or had they had competent leadership, the British Empire in India would have come to a swift and inglorious end. The British, however, quelled this uprising with brutal force, but it shook them to their roots. The British subsequently declared the Poorabiya (Eastern) troops of UP, Bihar and Bengal, with the help of which they had conquered the bulk of India, as non-martial and stopped their recruitment into the British Indian Army. The entire recruiting bias was shifted to the Punjab—to the Sikh and Punjabi Musalman troops who had largely remained loyal to the Raj. Also, a large number of Gurkha and hill troops regiments, like Kumaonis, Garhwalis and Dogras were now recruited to keep the people of the Indo-Gangetic plains under check. The new Indian army was raised on segmented ethnic lines to ensure that they would never subscribe to the idea of India. Their primary attempt thereafter was to sanitise their British Indian Army and ensure that it remained loyal to the Raj. That is why its entire recruitment focus was diverted to the Punjab and the Hill tribes (Gurkhas, Garhwalis, Kumaonis). The heavy emphasis on a Regimental System of motivation served the colonial design of accentuating local, ethnic and linguistic identities and preventing the crystallisation of a "Pan-Indian" identity that the nationalists were so desperately trying to forge. The only flaw in this thesis was that in times of war and rapid expansion (as in the two wars) this narrow manpower base of the martial classes completely broke down and had to be supplemented by recruiting thousands of soldiers from clans and castes declared non-martial by the British. Thus, in these wars the British were forced to recruit the Mazhbi Sikhs, Mahars and Biharis, etc.

Post 1857: British Divide & Rule Policies

This massive uprising eroded the carefully maintained façade that the Company ruled on behalf of the weak Mughal Emperor. Dr. Mithi Mukherjee writes in *India in the Shadows of Empire*, "the revolt underlined that significant parts of the Indian population, though seemingly hostile to one another, were capable of uniting against colonial rule. Force by itself would not suffice to maintain the empire. *If the British Empire had to survive in India, it had to find a way to overcome its foreignness as a source of provocation for future uprisings. It had, even more importantly, to destroy and dismantle all sources of Indian unity and identity—cultural, political and historical; and render the very idea of India as meaningless.*" She continues, "Torn by internal conflict, it was claimed that *India was in desperate need of a neutral and impartial power at the helm of the state to secure justice and order (or justice as order).* Given that Indian society was deeply divided into communities in conflict with each other, *only an alien, foreign power could be trusted to be neutral and impartial.*" Thus was laid the ideological basis for persistent foreign rule in India that lasted two centuries. The concept of Imperial Justice was specifically created to justify foreign rule in a deeply divided and fractured Indian society. Dr. Mithi Mukherjee writes, "*For India to have any order and unity, the state would have to be exterior to the civil society and nation.* It was this intervention of the discourse of Imperial Justice, coupled with state's representation of India as a deeply divided society that tried to turn the exteriority and foreign origin of the colonial state into its greatest strength, rather than a weakness."

Thus came into being the *British imperial discourse of justice as equity*. Only a foreign and extrinsic power could deal impartially with the many warring sections of a deeply divided Indian society. Hence foreign rule was needed simply because Indian polity was so deeply fractured and incapable of governing itself. Only an external power could have enforced justice between communities.

Splintering India: The Colonial Construction of Caste

The primary aim of colonial rule therefore was to deeply fracture the Indian polity, and exploit every cultural, religious, ethnic and linguistic faultline in its society. One such colonial tool was the accentuation of caste in Indian society. *This was done by the British through the mechanism of Caste-based Census of the Indian population.* Mukherjee writes, "The British ratified caste by means of various colonial instruments such as district manuals, Gazettes, imperial surveys and finally the Census of 1872; and made *Varna*, the hierarchical ordering of castes into four groups as the central idea behind classification of Indian society." She adds, *"The census administration was driven by the ideological need to naturalise the absence of national unity and then institutionalise it by integrating it into routine administrative decisions and policies."*

Sir John Seeley, the author of the first census wrote, "The mutiny was in great measure put down by *turning the races of India against each other*. So long as this can be done, the government of India from England is possible. But, if this were to change and *should the population be moulded into a single nationality, we would have to leave.*" Risley rubbed it in further by saying, "Indians do not have the capacity to develop an idea of nationality, let alone rule themselves." He ascribed it primarily to the institution of caste. "*So long as a regime of castes persists, it is difficult to see how the sentiments of unity and solidarity can penetrate and inspire all classes of the community.*"

This polarisation of caste was begun as the pursuit of social justice and was the primary colonial mechanism for splintering and dividing the Indian population, of which the Hindus then constituted some 80%.

Community based Electorates

Subsequently the colonial administration tried to deepen these social cleavages and faultlines, by instituting separate electorates based upon religion and caste. Thus the Muslims were the first to get a separate electorate, and then the Christians, the Sikhs and also the Subaltern Castes (Dalits). Risley was a great proponent of separate electorates based upon religion and caste to thoroughly divide the Indian population.

As a counterpoise the primary effort of the subsequent nationalist movement in India was to craft a pan-Indian identity, beyond the pale of religion, community, language and caste. This sense of unity was strengthened by the mass mobilisation of Gandhi's freedom movement and persisted for a time even in the initial Nehruvian phase. The great pity is that, post-independence, *politics in India sought to revive the divisions and faultlines of caste and creed as a primary mechanism for mobilising voters. To secure narrow vote banks, based on promises of affirmative action for select caste groups, the Indian elections were turned into a referendum of segmented mobilisations based on caste. This segmented mobilisation created a virtual "communism of caste" that militated against merit and equity, and deeply splintered the Indian psyche once more in the post-colonial period.*

The Freedom Movement

The surprising fact about the freedom movement in India was that its leadership was predominantly composed of lawyers. They strongly supported the British colonial concept of imperial justice as equity. *They did not consider freedom a right but a privilege that the British imperial monarch would gift to her subjects. Such an attitude stems from the a priori acceptance that Indian society was hopelessly divided and at war with itself. As such, the ends of justice demanded that an extrinsic power enforce justice in an impartial and detached manner. India had to be ruled from without. Foreign rule was the only antidote to India's innate divisions and fragmentations.* Their mode of seeking "Home Rule" from the British was entirely premised upon pleading and petitioning the imperial monarch for justice against the colonial administration. The Freedom Movement was begun by this Anglophile club of Indian lawyers, petitioning and pleading the monarch as a small group of educated elite, on behalf of the subject Indian people. Their goal was home rule and they could never envision the idea of complete freedom.

Thus the Congress had been formed in 1885 by Allan Octavian Hume, an Englishman, and W. C. Bonnerjee, its first President, as a kind of an effete debating society where the natives would be taught the fundamentals of a guided democracy of sorts. Legally they drew inspiration from the trial of Warren Hastings when the crown in England had interceded on behalf of her subjects to deal with an errant administration in India. So all appeals of this effete Club of rich Indian Lawyers were addressed to her Royal Majesty the Queen against the local administration and its perceived misrule. There was no question of asking for freedom or ever questioning the power of the British monarch. The furthest they would go is Home Rule. They would thus address petitions to her royal highness, beseeching her benevolence to set right the wrongs perpetuated by her local, mindless minions. These petitions were couched in such slavish and ingratiating language that it would make the skin of any self-respecting people crawl. That was all these effete debating societies could do. The lawyers as a class dominated this system and set themselves up as the elite who would plead with the king emperor to seek favours for the Indian people. That was all that the early Congress was all about.

The British success *in completely splintering the Indian population was evident during the years of the First World War, when there was no rebellion in India even as the bulk of the British Indian Army was deployed overseas.* British Intelligence (the highly professional, IB) had thoroughly penetrated the Ghadar Movement of revolutionaries based in Canada and USA and foiled all their ambitious plots to stir an uprising in India during the war. A branch of the Ghadarites had planned to march on India via the East (as the INA would do during the Second World War). India had contributed some 1.3 million Indian soldiers and 146 million pounds to the war effort. Some 72,000 Indian soldiers laid down their lives and 11 received the Victoria Cross—the highest gallantry award in the empire.

Service in such large Armies has a homogenising impact and it somehow revived the moribund idea of India. These troops served overseas as part of the British Indian Army. They were organised in Indian divisions as corporate entities. They fought as equals and were lionised in Europe. They heard the slogans of liberty, fraternity and equality, and saw their colonial masters in dire straits in the trenches of France and Flanders. They fought and prevailed against the European soldiers (Germans, Austrians and Turks). It was a transformative experience for some 1.3 million troops from the Punjab and Northern parts of India. The least they expected from the British at the end of this war was gratitude and perhaps some form of home rule. The response was one of callous racism. In 1919, what they got was the massacre of Jallianwala Bagh.

The Second Strand of the Freedom Struggle: Gandhian Non-Violence

Jallianwala Bagh forms a major watershed in the Indian Freedom Struggle. It was Gandhi who plugged into the deep sense of outrage amongst the Indian people. He took charge of the Congress and turned it into a genuine instrument of mass-based but passive resistance. He mobilised the rural masses of India and banned practising lawyers from joining the non-cooperation movement launched in 1920. He broke free from the lawyers' discourse of pleading and petitioning the imperial monarch for home rule. He asked for genuine freedom or *Poorna Swarajya.* He turned the non-cooperation movement into a mass-based mobilisation that went out of the towns, reached out to and mobilised the Indian peasantry. This really electrified the nation. As in Mao's China, the nationalist movement was now based not on the industrial proletariat in the cities and towns but upon the peasants in the countryside. Gandhi sought to subsume religious differences by espousing the Muslim causes of the Khilafat, etc. However, he kept the movement strictly non-violent and propagated a renunciative form of freedom—so much more in tune with the traditional Indian concepts of *Moksha* and *Nirvana,* that went beyond identity per se into the amorphous universality of the Brahman, as it were. This mass mobilisation was highly successful in reaching out to the Indian masses and deepening the idea of India. Gandhi, however, kept insisting that the movement be kept non-violent. It appears that the British Administration felt, at a point of time, that this non-violent resistance would not pose a decisive threat to British rule in India. They could, they felt, have easily contained this non-violent movement and, therefore, they even tacitly encouraged it, by permitting it to gain a high media profile amongst the print and radio mediums of that period. They were understandably keen that the struggle for Indian independence should not turn violent and grim. The year 1857 was their enduring civilisational nightmare and they did not want any replay or repetition. It is now evident, from hindsight, that the British tacitly encouraged this non-violent, persuasive form of protest because they were convinced that it was not going to basically endanger their colonial rule. The extensive press coverage given to Mahatma Gandhi and his non-violent freedom movement based on peaceful demonstrations, fasts and *dharnas*, was designed to release the pent up energy of popular dissatisfaction with colonial rule but at the same time, prevent it from turning very violent. That violence would have endangered the colonial dispensation. *Non-violence did not, and hence it was tolerated.* It only served to establish the liberal credentials of British rule, its levels of enlightenment and actually reinforced its legitimacy to rule a very heterogeneous population where the natives, they averred, were not capable of ruling themselves.

So even while the Congress tom-tommed its nationalist credentials and abhorrence of colonial rule, they openly admired the British system and were in turn seen by the colonial masters as "Brown Sahibs" and closet Anglophiles in a nationalist disguise—*who were very convenient tools for the perpetuation of the Raj.* In the racial terms of that era, they were WOGs (an acronym for Western Oriented Gentlemen). In actual fact, however, as stated, wogs was the second half of "Golliwogs," a pejorative racial term of abuse which meant a Black Doll. These non-violent protests, therefore, acted as a safety valve for the popular sentiments and prevented the outbreak of large-scale violence in India.

The Third Strand of the Freedom Struggle: Violence of Bose and His Indian National Army (INA)

The third strand in the Indian movement for independence was led by Netaji Subhash Chandra Bose and his INA and the earlier revolutionaries like Bhagat Singh, Chandrashekhar Azad, Rajguru, etc. Bose was convinced that non-violence was completely within the tolerance thresholds of the Empire. He very correctly identified the loyalty of Indian sepoys as the Key Centre of Gravity of the Colonial Empire. The only Indian in the National Congress who could really challenge the overriding authority of the Mahatma was Subhash Chandra Bose. He was a realist. *He clearly foresaw that non-violence was absolutely within the tolerance thresholds of the colonial regime. This could mount media and psychological pressure but never of an order which would really compel the British to leave.* After the First World War, the demobilised 1.3 million strong body of the native Indian soldiers of the British Indian Army had really spread the ideas of nationalism in India, especially into the villages and countryside from which the peasant soldiers came. *Gandhiji had harvested this into a mass movement but carefully directed it into non-violent channels that would not strain the tolerance thresholds of the Empire, and only add to its feel-good factor of being a liberal regime, open to public pressure and persuasion—but only up to a point.* That point stopped well short of complete independence for India.

World War II had started in 1939. This time India had contributed a staggering 2.5 million men —the largest all-volunteer Army in the history of the world—an Army raised without conscription. Unwittingly, it was this that really deepened the idea of India. Once again large corporate bodies of Indian soldiers fought overseas as Indian divisions, thus unwittingly strengthening the idea of India as a pan-Indian identity beyond the narrow confines of caste and creed. The steady Indianisation of the officers' corps deepened this idea of India even further, and also sharpened the bitterness against racism in the ranks of the Army and its officers' messes and clubs. Gymkhana and other upper crust clubs in India in those days had boards at the entrance which proclaimed, "Indians and dogs not allowed." It was this racism that would cost the British their empire.

Bose differed radically from Gandhi. For him, the war presented a golden opportunity to reach out to the enemies of Britain, to Germany and Japan, and seek their help to free India. Gandhi opposed this realist mode of thought. Bose was completely marginalised in the Congress. Gandhi ensured that he did not become President of the Congress for a second term. Single-handedly, however, Bose escaped to Germany and there raised the Indische Legion (Indian Legion)—a brigade size force formed from the Indian prisoners of war. He was dismayed however by Hitler's racism. Meanwhile, the Japanese had gained spectacular success in the Asia-Pacific theatre. They had raised an Indian National Army from the prisoners of war they held. They were having problems managing it and they asked the Germans for Bose. The Germans took 13 long months to transfer him.

Finally, Bose undertook a perilous voyage by Sea in a German U-boat. Off the course of Madagascar, Bose transferred to a Japanese submarine and reached Japan. He deeply impressed Prime Minister Tojo and the top Japanese leadership with his transparent sincerity. He established the Provisional Government of Azad Hind and declared War on Britain. He expanded the INA to a respectable size of 1,500 officers and 60,000 men, and organised them in three divisions. Some 26,000 of these perished in the battles of Imphal and Kohima and the subsequent retreat through Burma. The INA lost the battles but won the War for Independence. After the war, in a misplaced gesture of triumphalism, the British put on trial 9 INA officers at the iconic Red Fort of Delhi. The intent was to rub salt into the Indian wounds. It enraged the people of India. Worse, it triggered widespread mutinies in the Royal Indian Navy, the Royal Indian Air Force and many units of the British Indian Army. The British were truly shaken to their core. Some 2.5 million men of the British Indian Army were then being demobilised post World War II, and they were angry and enraged. The British saw the writing on the wall. Their white troops were tired, war-weary and homesick. They had no stomach for taking on some 2.5 million armed men of the Indian Army or large parts thereof. They decided to quit with grace and left within two years after the end of World War II. The sun had finally set on the British Empire.

Thus, what had brought about the end of the empire really were the INA and the Indian Armed Forces. The First War of Independence had been waged by the Indian soldiers of the Presidency armies in 1857. The British had gone all out to fragment Indian society thereafter. It was the mass mobilisations of World War I and World War II that coincidentally reinforced the idea of India through the mammoth British Indian Armed Forces that were raised to fight overseas wars as an organisational entity that was Indian in essence. The Indian Army numbered 1.3 million in the First World War and a staggering 2.5 million in the Second World War. It is my contention that these mammoth, pan-Indian organisations revived the historical idea of India and, unwittingly, nurtured the trampled Indian identity. The first step towards nation building is to raise strong national armed forces to protect that state and give it the monopoly of violence.

The British unwittingly prompted the impulse towards nationalism by raising these huge National Armed Forces as corporate entities with a life and sub-culture of their own. It was these armed forces in the end that offered violent resistance to the colonial rule and forced the British to leave. The INA played a pivotal role and was instrumental in getting India her freedom. The sacrifice of 26,000 men (or even less, but a significant number) cannot be termed as a non-violent struggle. The very example of these men, who fought as Indians to free India, resuscitated the dying idea of India, and virtually caused a second revolt in the Indian Armed Forces. It was this impending second revolt that caused the Empire to unravel. Bose and his INA had managed to shake the loyalty of the Indian soldiers towards the Raj and this was a major feat. The central idea of the Bose thesis was to subvert and transform the organisational culture of these vast all-volunteer Armed Forces that the British had raised in India, and turn the primary instruments of British subjugation and control against them.

The wily British had seen the writing on the wall. They left, but before that, they cleverly "transferred power" to the Anglophile coterie of lawyers in the Nehru-led Congress. These lawyers soon marginalised Gandhi and buried Bose. They revived the discourse of imperial justice by adopting the British India Act of 1935 virtually as our Constitution and enshrined *justice* as the most important ideal of the Constitution. Mukherjee says, "*these lawyers made justice the basic foundation of the Indian Constitution.* The other instrument of Imperial Justice —the Imperial Monarch—soon manifested itself in the dynastic leadership of the Congress, now represented by the Nehru-Gandhi family, which continued to be a powerful force in Indian politics till 2014, when it was decimated in the recent parliamentary elections, Mukherjee writes:

Once, the British had left, the Congress by sheer force of the habit of the discourse of imperial justice as equity, slowly had begun to elevate one of their own, Jawaharlal Nehru, to occupy the imperial position of monarch as imperial judge. Parliament (largely the Congress), now configured itself as a court of equity centred on Nehru as the new monarch. The emergence of the Nehru-Gandhi dynasty was a derivative of the British discourse of justice as equity. Nehru, the agnostic, was the secular monarch of this state, yet stood aloof and apart, as its new, extrinsic monarch to give justice to its perpetually warring communities and castes.

The Nehruvian Narrative of State

From the point of view of national security, Nehru now crafted a deliberate Narrative of State for India. To downplay the violent resistance of INA and the revolt of the Indian Armed Forces that had finally secured independence, Nehru propagated the patent falsehood that India had secured her independence entirely by non-violent means and methods. As such, force, he felt, had no role to play whatsoever in the birth and establishment of the Indian Republic. Nehru claimed that among the entire comity of Westphalian nation states (based on the sole monopoly of violence), India was an exceptional state—as it was not based on hard power—but the soft power of *Ahimsa, Satyagraha, Non-violence,* etc. This was patently incorrect as it refused to factor in the pivotal role of the INA and the subsequent mutinies it had instigated. Nevertheless, in his bid to marginalise Bose, Nehru strenuously built up this narrative of state and went to inordinate lengths to ingrain it in the national psyche. In keeping with the Indian states allegedly pacific origins, he claimed that India did not need Armed Forces, that only police forces would suffice. He refused to rehabilitate the INA personnel and denied them their wartime pensions.

Nehruvian Paradox

Nehru thus created a paradox. All Westphalian nation states are based on a monopoly of hard power. Disputes between nations are still resolved by the use of force. As a lawyer, Nehru now elevated the imperial concept of justice and ascribed its preservation to the newly formed United Nations Organisation (UNO), and felt that it would need lawyers like him to plead and petition the new Global Body of supranational justice. Armed Forces had no role whatsoever. It was only the Realists like Patel who prevented him from damaging and disbanding these inherited institutions. In any case, India had to threaten the use of force to make the princely states accede to the Union of India, and make India a cohesive and contiguous state and not a quilt patchwork of local fiefdoms. Patel threatened to march in the Indian Army into any princely state that refused to accede to India. The princes saw the writing on the wall and caved in tamely. It was Patel's assertive use of the instruments of military force that really served to unify India and make it a cohesive and governable entity.

The Post-Independence Narrative

The immediate challenges to India came in J&K and Hyderabad and in both Patel marched in the Army despite Nehru's reservations and Hamlet-like indecision. Nehru subsequently tried to assert himself and took the case of Kashmir to the UNO. It was a disastrous decision and India is still paying for that folly. Patel unfortunately died early and Nehru soon had his way. *Nehru arrogated to himself the role of peacemaker of the planet. This construct was initially fashionable in a war-weary world, and for a time allowed India to punch much above her weight in the various world fora. Neutrality was elevated to the level of dogma—in terms of Non-Alignment. India sent peacekeeping missions to all conflict spots of the world. India adopted a highly preachy and moralist tone in its international discourse as it touted the values of Ahimsa and Satyagraha to an increasingly violent world. Nehru ensconced himself as the new global messiah of peace and non-violence.* The whole of Bollywood was now pressed into service for an information warfare offensive of impressive proportions. Film after film being churned out of Bollywood extolled India as a kind of a haven of universal peace and harmony, designed to bring peace and solicitude to a warring world. Nehru was built up as a great world statesman preaching peace to a constantly warring world.

In 1956, the military coup happened in Pakistan. This made Nehru paranoid. He now completely marginalised the military and used the bureaucracy and Intelligence services to cut it to size. Its Generals were pushed down in the order of precedence and marginalised from all decision-making process. Nehru treated the military contemptuously, as the last outpost of the Raj, and tried to tame it by eroding its professionalism and promoting sycophants and relations to key positions. Worst of all, he completely starved it of resources. India reduced its defence expenditure to just around one per cent of its GDP. This soft power mindset led to the disaster of 1962, when China taught India a humiliating lesson in realpolitik. Nehru turned hysterical and sought western military intervention. It was only a tactical defeat but *the spectacle of collapse in the soft state was most unedifying and disgraceful. Nehru, with his inordinate emphasis on soft power, had created a very weak state, incapable of defending itself or using military force to effect critical outcomes in terms of national security.* Such weakness could imperil its independent existence. *It was a state that deliberately chose not to think in strategical or National security terms.* The initial defence of the India-China border was assigned to the Police forces and the attempt was to *build the Police as some sort of counterpoise to the untrustworthy military.*

The Onset of Realism

The 1962 debacle did occasion a significant course correction in India. Nehru died heartbroken but his successors had learnt a bitter lesson in realism. The Indian Armed Forces were rapidly expanded and modernised. The 1965 War caught them half-way in their modernisation process. However, it did give them very valuable hands-on professional experience. Russia stepped in, in a major way thereafter, to subsidise the Indian military build-up. They provided India the cutting-edge military technology of that era. By 1971, India had arrived as a strong regional power. It broke Pakistan into two and formed a new nation state with the force of arms. The Bangladesh war was a decisive tri-service blitzkrieg that saw a march on an enemy capital, mass surrender of armies (93,000 prisoners of war) and enforced regime change. For the first time after the Second World War, a new nation had been created by the force of arms. By 1974 Indira Gandhi had tested a nuclear weapon. India had arrived on the world stage as a major military power.

The first oil shock of 1973, however, had derailed the Indian political economy and eroded Indira Gandhi's political legitimacy. A Gandhian mass movement was unleashed against her by Jayaprakash Narayan (JP). *Dr Mukherjee says that the Congress's attempt to make an imperial monarch out of its leadership, in the form of Nehru-Gandhi dynasty, was now countered by the second strain of the Freedom Movement—Gandhian mass mobilisation.* In the face of this mass movement led by a Gandhian, Jayaprakash Narayan, Indira Gandhi panicked. Goaded by her inordinately ambitious younger son, Sanjay, she imposed the highly unpopular national emergency. This saw the rout of Smt. Indira Gandhi in the 1977 parliamentary elections. However, the neo-Gandhian dispensation that followed was a weak and motley coalition that unravelled within two years.

Indira Gandhi returned to power and, with Soviet assistance, greatly strengthened the Indian Armed Forces. She was an ardent nationalist and had used Pakistan as the *hostile other* to generate a nationalist consolidation. The Western powers felt threatened by her muscular nationalism. The Afghan War had started and Pakistan had become a key frontline state for the CIA's jihad against the Soviet Army. The Sikh terrorist movement for Khalistan was instigated in the Punjab, to keep India preoccupied and enable Pakistan's army to focus on Afghanistan. All the communities that had been given separate electorates by the British, to give salience to their separate identities, were fully exploited in the post-colonial phase by the foreign intelligence organisations to instigate insurgencies/local rebellions in India. Indira Gandhi was a charismatic and nationalist leader who was making India a strong regional power with growing ambitions. The West was distinctly unhappy with her muscular brand of nationalism. They were alarmed over the ruthless way in which she had broken Pakistan into two and then exploded a peaceful nuclear device. It is no secret that in the 1980s Indira Gandhi was spoiling for a fight with Pakistan to pay it back for instigating terror in the Punjab.

Indira Gandhi was assassinated on October 31, 1984. Her tech-savvy elder son, Rajiv Gandhi, took over with a massive sympathy mandate, but soon frittered it away in pandering to all manner of pressure groups. The Nehru-Gandhi dynasty as an imperial-monarchical surrogacy institution was fast losing steam. Rajiv Gandhi was assassinated on May 22, 1992 and India now stepped into an era of weak and unstable coalition governments based on the fractured mandates of identity politics.

The Bharatiya Janata party now started a Hindu majoritarian mobilisation with the Ayodhya Ram Temple movement. To counter it, the then Prime Minister, V. P. Singh, took a leaf straight out of the colonial armoury of divisive instruments. He dusted out caste to deeply fracture and splinter the Hindu community and prevent its consolidation as a vote bank. *He justified it as the sole way to promote justice between castes and creeds and thereby secure secularism.* The social justice card of the colonial era was now taken out by the political leadership of post-colonial India, and a second fracturing programme to splinter the pan-Indian identity was now unleashed after 1857, this time by the *Indians themselves.* The entire state machinery was pressed in to sharpen caste identities and *promise indiscriminate affirmative action on the basis of caste and creed markers. Economic price tags were now put on identity markers now by the device of reservation.* In a bizarre move, 50% of the Indian population was brought into the ambit of caste-based reservations. The entire nationalist project of the freedom struggle, to carve out a pan-Indian identity beyond caste and creed, was thus virtually destroyed.

Identity Politics

What followed thereafter was an era of most petty and divisive, identity-based politics based on caste-mobilisation of a degree that would have left the British colonial regime envious. India outdid her former colonial masters in fracturing and splintering itself and descending into the tribalism of caste. Romila Thapar, a prime courtier of the Nehru-Gandhi dynasty, emerged as the chief theoretician of this new ideology of social justice and equity based on the politics of caste. This Queen of caste proclaimed that there was no religion like Hinduism, only a conglomeration of *jatis* and castes. To prevent a consolidation of the majority of Indian population, the colonial card of caste had been invoked with a splintering intent that was odious and surprising in the lengths to which its proponents might have gone.

The second Oil Shock of 1990 meanwhile completely derailed the Indian economy. The then Prime Minister, P.V. Narsimha Rao, was now forced to rapidly liberalise the Indian economy and dismantle the license-permit Raj to enable the private sector in India to take its economy to the next level. This unleashed the entrepreneurial energies of India's corporate sector. This was also the stage in which the Ayodhya Ram temple agitation peaked. It was the BJP's counter to the bid to fracture the Hindu vote along the faultlines of caste and somehow consolidate a majoritarian vote bank to counter the use of the minorities as a captive vote bank.

Dowager Empress

Sonia Gandhi, the Italian widow of Rajiv Gandhi, was now cast into the role of the new Dowager Empress of India. The justice as equity discourse of the colonial era was revived with a new fervour. Only a white-skinned foreigner could be impartial and neutral in the squabbles between India's multiplicity of castes and creeds. Sonia was now elevated to the status of the new queen empress of the Congress, and thereby of India per se. Congress won the elections and Manmohan Singh was made the figurehead Prime Minister to administer the state on Sonia's behalf. Sonia, as the president of the Congress, was the real monarch and thus a diarchy form of government with dual power centres came into being in New Delhi. Sonia's National Advisory Council (NAC) of Leftist-Liberal intellectuals goaded her to policies that would keep the bulk of Indians hopelessly poor and dependent solely on the doles and freebies tossed by the new Empress of India. India had revived the colonial discourse with a new vehemence that was astonishing. How could a free nation regress so thoroughly to the colonial modes of governance? This unleashed a tyranny of short-term agendas, based on buying captive vote-banks through freebies, doles and targeted affirmative action based on caste/identity markers. Accentuating these tendencies were Sonia's possible subterranean support to agendas of proselytisation aimed at converting large segments of the neglected tribal populations, who were consciously prevented from modernising and entering the national mainstream. This spate of freebies coupled with the Oil Shock of 2013 derailed the Indian economy once again, for the third time in succession, much on the lines that a profligate welfare state had derailed the Greek economy.

The two competing ideologies in India were the discourse of social justice as equity with a foreign national as Queen Empress or Monarch—the impartial outsider, ensuring justice and equity between the perpetually warring castes and creeds; and the Bharatiya Janata Party (BJP), on the other hand, which was attempting a national consolidation based upon consolidating the 80% majority of Hindus. The social justice discourse was doing its bit to splinter the Hindu vote into a multiplicity of caste segments and thereby marginalise the majority community of the country entirely by reducing it to competing and hostile caste alignments. Pushed beyond a point, this marginalisation alarmed and angered the Hindu majority. From around 2008-13, the Rashtriya Swayamsewak Sangh (RSS) and its affiliate organisations attempted to create a right wing consolidation—a revival of nationalism as it were. The image of Bharat Mata seated on a lion now began to emerge in most street corners of mofussil towns of North India. The build-up to 2014 had begun. A hard right Hindu Government finally emerged from these elections with an overwhelming majority in parliament.

Three Strands of the Freedom Struggle

To understand India's present, therefore, and to determine where the nation state is headed, *it is highly essential for us to deconstruct our recent history. We must understand the seamlessness of connectivity in our pre- and post-colonial narratives that emerge from the way India was colonised and then how precisely it got its freedom.* We need to understand the three distinct strands that emerged in the course of our freedom struggle. These are:

- The discourse of imperial justice as equity, practised by the Anglophile lawyers who remained craven subjects of the empire. Their method was to plead and petition the monarch for Home Rule.
- The discourse of renunciative politics as practised by Mahatma Gandhi through a mass mobilisation of the rural folk. This strand of mass-mobilisation movements re-emerged post-Emergency as the JP Movement, and later the Anna Hazare Movement against corruption in 2012-13.
- The third strand was that of violent Armed Resistance. It had first broken out amongst the British Indian Armed Forces in 1857, and then in the form of the revolutionaries like Bhagat Singh, Chandra Shekhar Azad and Rash Bihari Bose finally culminated in the form of the INA from 1942 to 1945. It culminated in the subsequent mutinies it inspired in the British Indian Armed Forces in 1946. The year 1857 had come very close to overthrowing the British. The INA, however, actually got us our freedom by inspiring physical mutinies in the Royal Indian Navy, the British Indian Army and the Royal Indian Air Force in the immediate wake of World War II. That is the historical truth about India's freedom.

Patterns of the Past

These, then, are the *patterns that tie our pre-colonial history with the post-colonial developments. Modern Indian History also clearly highlights the coincidence of oil price shocks with deep-seated dislocations of the Indian political economy. Three oil shocks have triggered three major political crises in India in 1973-75, 1990 and 2014.* Dislocation of the political economy delegitimises the ruling elite and in the Indian case, dislocated the imperial justice discourse through the medium of Gandhian mass mobilisation in movements like the one triggered by JP in 1977 and Anna Hazare in 2013-14. It is important for us to recognise that the Colonial empire did not grant India independence. They "transferred power" to a coterie of Anglophile lawyers who continued with the ideology of imperial justice as equity by enshrining Justice as the cornerstone virtually of the Indian Constitution. The Indian Constitution was largely a codification of the British India Act of 1935. Its cornerstone remained the fact that India was such a heterogeneous mixture of warring castes and creeds that some external agency was needed to ensure justice and equity between its feuding communities. This role was performed by the British Queen Empress in the Colonial period. It was taken over by the Nehru-Gandhi dynasty in the post-colonial period. Whenever oil shocks destabilised the Indian political economy, the Ruling Nehru Gandhi dynasty was overthrown with the help of Gandhian style mass movements like the ones led by JP in the 1970s and by Anna Hazare in 2013-14, as also the RSS inspired upsurge of Right Wing Nationalism that culminated in the Modi victory of 2014. Those are the patterns that emerge from an analysis of our recent pre- and post-colonial history.

3

The Abject Failure of the Quit India Movement of Mahatma Gandhi

Null Hypothesis

Having taken an overview of the entire freedom struggle let us now revert to the question which we had posed at the outset of this book. Who really was instrumental in getting India its Freedom—Bose or Mahatma Gandhi? If we have to proceed empirically, it would be essential to employ a null hypothesis. To settle the question of who got us our freedom it would be essential to first examine the final push of the Congress towards freedom that took place in the Form of the Quit India Movement in 1942. This was the final and allegedly decisive phase of the peaceful freedom struggle of Gandhi. So, did it succeed? It would be essential to examine how it fared for that alone can help us to settle this historical debate in a logical fashion. The simple fact is that though it was Mahatma Gandhi who had initially forced Bose out of the National Congress and virtually forced him to leave India, towards the mid-point of the Second World War, both men had developed a sneaking admiration for one another. Bose had called Gandhi the Father of the Nation because of his undisputed role in graduating the freedom struggle in India from the old-style effete debating clubs of the original Congress to a mass-based grass-roots movement that Gandhi had spread to the villages. He had involved the Indian peasantry to make it a genuine grass-roots movement with mass participation. After Bose had left India, Gandhi openly admired his courage, will power and tenacity of purpose. As time went on, he increasingly began to veer towards Bose's view that the British would not leave unless they were really forced to go. The tragic experience of World War I clearly indicated how ungrateful they could be after the war was won. Even Gandhi realised, as time went on, that World War II presented a rare and unique opportunity for India to make an all-out attempt to win her freedom. This presented a narrow window of time in which to act and this would last only as long as the war lasted.

Polarisation in the Congress

We now see a distinct and disturbing polarisation within the Congress. Even as Mahatma Gandhi veered around to Bose's view of a now or never chance to win freedom, Nehru was increasingly inclined to go along with the British. In fact, he went so far as to proclaim that if Bose was to come to India with the Japanese invading armies he would personally go forward to fight him. This was noted by the astute British and after the Quit India Movement they began an all-out attempt to completely marginalise Gandhi and rely more and more on Nehru. By the time of independence, the marginalisation of the Mahatma was sadly total and complete. Let us therefore take a more detailed look at the Quit India Movement of 1942 for it was truly the last charge of the Congress, and it would be necessary to evaluate its outcome and results.

Quit India Movement: August 1942

To placate the Americans who were pressurising Britain to make up with the Congress, Churchill had sent the Cripps Mission in early April 1942 with a virtual plan for the partition of India. This was rejected by the Congress. Secretary of State L. S. Amery felt that Nehru and Azad would break with Gandhi and help the British in their war against Japan, despite the Congress's rejection of the Cripps proposals in April 1942. In fact, Nehru had told a meeting at Guwahati on April 24, 1942 that he would "fight Mr. Subhash Bose and his party along with Japan, if he comes to India." Azad was noticing a clear hardening of Mahatma Gandhi's position and how he was veering around completely to Netaji's point of view on how India should fight for its freedom.

Gandhi now openly admired Bose's courage in escaping to Germany. Gandhi felt the time had come to "Do or Die." Despite reservations expressed by Nehru, Azad and others, he insisted on launching the Quit India Movement. In fact, Gandhiji's draft resolution sent to the Congress Working Committee had demanded immediate cessation of British Rule in India. This was precisely the position that Bose had urged him to take in his last meeting in the Wardha session in 1940. Miffed by Gandhi's new found truculence, the British had apparently been working on Nehru. Amery, the British Secretary of State had in fact said, "*There is reasonable hope that the Congress led by Nehru will at any rate try to help in its own curious fashion in opposing Japanese aggression*" (Sitanshu Das, p. 520). Nehru and Azad however initially quailed at such a level of collaboration. They were still in awe of Gandhiji and finally they went along with him to launch the Quit India Movement in August 1942. Clearly Nehru was in no position then to strike out on his own and defy Gandhiji at this juncture.

The August 4, 1942 the Congress Working Committee (CWC) Resolution was forced to take a hardline position. It asked for immediate cessation of British Rule in India. Churchill was furious. As Bose had noted, restlessness was spreading in India. The CWC could not have continued with the policy of drift after the British War Cabinet refused to improve upon the Cripps proposal which the Congress had rejected. So, the Quit India Movement was launched. Gandhi was arrested and his last message was, "We get our Freedom or we Die (*Karo ya Maro*)."

Churchill was livid. He was always full of venom against the "beastly Indians and their beastly religion." He told the British Cabinet, "We must not sell India to the Hindu priesthood and the Congress caucus." Churchill in fact was ready to lose India temporarily to the Axis invaders rather than concede dominion status to "non-white" India. It is noteworthy that Nehru, Azad, Rajagopalachari, Sarojini Naidu, Syed Muhammad and Asif Ali—all members of the CWC had expressed reservations about the Quit India Resolution. Because of Mahatma Gandhi's prestige and stature, however, they were forced to go along. The British displayed no qualms or reservations, however, in crushing this movement as brutally as they could. Gandhiji's fasts were now of no avail. Churchill hated him anyway and was not bothered if he passed away in prison.

Military Reaction to Quit India Movement

In August 1942, to suppress the Quit India Movement of Mahatma Gandhi, the British used a total of eight Brigades with some fifty-seven and a half battalions for a period of 6 to 8 weeks. These were all-white troops of British or allied extraction. Viceroy Linlithgow reported to Churchill that "*this was the most serious rebellion since 1857, the gravity of which we have so far concealed from the world due to reasons of military security.*" To aid this revolt, Bose had sent gold, US dollars, radio sets and arms to India. Talwar and his gang of traitors, however, left most of these at the Soviet Embassy in Kabul. This was not given to the associates of Bose and the money was divided between Talwar and the Kirti/CPI workers (Sitanshu Das). The Quit India Movement thus entirely petered out. All the Congress leadership was clapped in jail and draconian wartime censorship ensured that the Freedom Movement was completely deprived of the oxygen of media publicity. Within two months, it was all over for the Quit India Movement of the Congress, bar the shouting. The British had been brutal and ruthless and the Non-Violent Movement collapsed entirely in the face of such draconian and repressive measures. In the face of a brutal and determined military power non-violence had unfortunately failed entirely for it is primarily directed at a status quo regime with some humanist and liberal values. As an American military writer put it recently, faced with a Stalinist kind of ruthless repression, "Gandhi dies" before a firing squad or in a brutal Gulag.

So, does the Gandhian form of mass mobilisation and non-violent protest lack efficacy? The simple fact is that in the post-war period Gandhian methods were followed by Martin Luther King in the United States itself with considerable success. The counterpoint is that the USA is a liberal democracy. Would this have worked in Stalin's Soviet Union or Hitler's Germany? Such mass mobilisations and non-violent protests however were repeated later in Eastern Europe via a series of Spring revolutions. Then we had the coloured revolutions in Europe and Central Asia and elsewhere, and then of course came the Arab Spring. In all these cases the ruling regimes were relatively not as tyrannical and ruthless and a collapse of the political economies of these countries had weakened the ruling dispensations and had led to widespread disaffection and unrest. and not just the masses but the police, military and other security agencies as well, were fairly demoralised. In recent times, Information Technology has facilitated mass mobilisation at a hitherto unprecedented pace. Internet and text messages can generate huge "Flash mobs" in a matter of days and hours. But how lasting are these effects? The Arab Spring in Egypt has since been reversed and the Army is back in charge. The jury however is still out on this larger issue. The historical fact is all African nations that adopted the non-violent methods for their Freedom Struggle only got their liberation from 1960-1970 onwards and even later. Nelson Mandela's South Africa finally got its freedom only as late as April 1994. *Had Bose not acted as he did, even India would have gotten its independence some 30-40 years after it finally did secure it in 1947 by the threat of military violence.*

Let us now however go back to the era of World War II to see how events panned out then. Let us not forget that in Churchill's time , India was faced with a rather ruthless regime that was at war, and had not batted an eyelid as 3 million Indians died of starvation, even as it destroyed all boats and country craft in the riverine terrain of what is now Bangladesh to prevent a Japanese invasion via the sea. It had also used some eight brigades of white troops to brutally suppress Mahatma Gandhi's Quit India movement. This was not a dispensation that would understand the language of Non-violence.

The Gandhi who came out of prison in 1944 seemed to be a broken man. Largely broken in health and spirit. He had undertaken fasts in prison and Churchill had menacingly said let him die. With wartime censorship in place they were confident they could handle the civil unrest that would follow Gandhi's death. They had after all just used the 57 white battalions to very good effect to crush whatever unrest that had followed. There was no second-tier Congress leadership that could guide a mass scale civilian unrest. Bose was making his broadcasts from Tokyo to guide the Indian people on the techniques of sabotage and subversion but his clandestine radio broadcasts had been banned and were not readily available to the mass of the Indian public. Sadly, all of Bose's attempts to smuggle in weapons and explosives and gold, etc., had been betrayed by double agents like Talwar. The Quit India movement had largely petered out.

However, even then, had the Japanese attacked in the summer of 1942 or even after the monsoons or even in 1943, they would have cut through like a knife through butter. The bulk of the British and white troops were involved in internal security duties inside India. Japan still had the edge in air power and naval power. By 1944 the tide had turned decisively with US intervention. The British had rebuilt a massive new Indian army. US support had given them air and naval superiority. By 1944 when the Japanese-INA offensive was launched it was a tragic case of too little too late. Despite the odds the Japanese almost pulled it off and the battles of Imphal-Kohima were the hardest fought battles of the British empire. By the monsoon of 1944, however, the danger was past. The Japanese logistical system collapsed in the monsoons and soon they and the INA were in a miserable retreat. The only thing that saved them from annihilation was just the formidable reputation of the Japanese Army. The British now felt confident that they could now release the incarcerated Congress leadership.

Statements of Mahatma Gandhi after His Release

Dr Kalyan Kumar De in his inimitable book, *Netaji Subhash: Liberator of Indian Subcontinent* has carried out invaluable research into the British Transfer of Power archives. He has uncovered a veritable treasure trove of excellent historical documents that clearly highlight with the help of authentic documentary evidence, that it was not the non- violent struggle of the Congress but the INA trials which had unleashed a wave of violence all over India and shaken the loyalty of the British Indian armed forces to the Raj that forced the British to panic and leave. As confirmatory evidence for the Failure of the Quit India movement, he has cited the statements of Mahatma Gandhi immediately after his release from jail in 1944. He repeatedly cites instances of Mahatma Gandhi saying that he had no more legal authority to carry on with the Quit India Movement and could not ask anyone to continue with the non-cooperation movement. In other words, the Quit India Movement was all over. This was the most tacit admission of defeat from the top leader of the Quit India Movement himself and is the final epitaph about the sad but abject failure of this non-violent movement. In the face of ruthless military action it just petered out and collapsed. The power of state coercion prevailed and the non-violent movement collapsed altogether. The first-hand statements of Mahatma Gandhi clearly highlight this caving in and collapse of the Quit India Movement. I will now cite the specific statements of Mahatma Gandhi quoted by Kalyan De. He has taken these excerpts from the Collected Works of Mahatma Gandhi.

Speech to Congressmen at Poona June 29, 1944

Gandhiji said: "today I do not meet you in any representative capacity. In terms of Sataygraha, the moment I was imprisoned I ceased to wield the authority reposed in me by Congress and if I am now out of prison, it is not because of my strength or yours but because of my illness... This fortuitous release does not restore to me the authority that lapsed with my imprisonment."

Interview with Stuart Gelder July 4, 1944 (*Bombay Chronicle*, July 13, 1944)

When Stuart asked him, "supposing you saw the Viceroy what would you say to him?" Gandhi replied, "I would tell him that I sought the interview *with a view to helping and not hindering the Allied war effort*. But I can do nothing without seeing the members of the Working Committee for I believe that my authority under the August resolution ended with my imprisonment. It was not revived by my release." Further he said in the interview, "history does not repeat itself. The conditions of 1942 do not exist today. The world has moved on during the last two years. The whole situation has to be renewed de novo. The point, therefore, for me to discuss with the Working Committee is to know how they react to the knowledge that I gained since my release." It is noteworthy that in 1942 when the bulk of the CWC had opposed the launch of the Quit India Movement, Gandhji had overridden their objections. Such was his prestige then that none could stand against him or question his authority then. These statements therefore mark a sad contrast.

Interview to Press, Panchgani, July 13, 1944

"What no one can do in the name of the Congress is mass civil disobedience, which was never started and which, as I have said, I cannot at the present moment, even in my personal capacity, start." This is a clear acknowledgement of defeat. Gandhi was most unwilling to ask for a resumption of the civil disobedience movement and after his release from jail strenuously denied any plans to relaunch it. He offered complex legal sounding arguments as to how he had, by virtue of his arrest, lost all authority and would have to have the views of the CWC before he could do or say anything at all. The Quit India Movement was largely over.

Talk to Bombay Congress Leaders, Panchgani, July 29-30, 1944

Gandhiji said, "9 August is a great day and it is the duty of all to observe it. But the part of the resolution which speaks of mass civil disobedience cannot be brought into force because the authority to put it in force vested solely in me. Today I see no possibility of mass civil disobedience either according to that authority or according to circumstances." This sadly is an admission of abject defeat. It was all over as far as the Quit India Movement was concerned and the do or die phase was all but finished.

Statement to the Press, Sevagram, August 5, 1944

Gandhiji said, "Many Congressmen asked me how to celebrate 9 August. That date was a turning point in India's fight for freedom. I had wanted to spend that date in peaceful introspection and to inaugurate negotiations for a peaceful settlement. But the Government or fate willed it otherwise. The Government went mad and so did some people. Sabotage and the like were resorted to and many things were done in the Congress name or in my name. I am aware that I do not represent the Congress mind always. Many Congressmen repudiate my Non-violence. The CWC is the only body which can legitimately and truly represent Congress."

Considering that the whole Working Committee in 1942 had serious reservations about launching the Quit India Movement and Gandhiji alone had brushed aside their objections and pushed the resolution through, it was a sad climb down. The British had broken his spirit in prison and possibly turned around many of the other Congress leaders then in incarceration. The entire Quit India Movement—the grand finale as it were of the non-violent struggle—had fizzled out without a whimper. If there is any doubt whatsoever of abject defeat it should be cleared by the last part of the statement of Mahatma Gandhi in 1944:

"The second thing that I should like done on the forthcoming 9th of August is for those who have gone underground to discover themselves. They can do so by informing the authorities of their movements and whereabouts or by simply and naturally doing their work in the open without any attempt to evade or elude the police. To go underground is to elude the police." This proclaims the end of all resistance to the British Colonial power and coming out of hiding and virtually surrendering to the Police. These slew of statements concede complete defeat and failure of the Brave Quit India Movement that has been tom-tommed as the last decisive charge of the non-violent brigade that really pushed out the British. All these statements do not suggest any victory.

They are sadly admissions of total failure and an abject sense of loss and control.

4

The Clement Attlee-Chakrabarty Dialogue

Identifying Key Decision Makers

In our efforts to resolve this historical debate about the reality of the formation of a post-colonial state in India, we will have to identify the key decision makers who shaped the British decision to quit India finally. Who were these key decision makers and what finally impelled them to make the choices that they did? What was weighing most upon their minds? Was it the cumulative pressure generated by decades of a pacific and non-violent Civil Disobedience Movement in India and the cumulative weight of the long and tortuous negotiations process? That is what Bipin Chandra and other court historians would have us believe. Or was it plain and simple the threat of a major military revolt instigated by the mass emotions aroused by the trial of INA officers? What finally worked? Hard power, the threat of a military revolt, or the soft power of non-violence and persuasion? It is vital to draw up this list of key British decision makers and then dispassionately examine their views and the actions taken by them at that time. The key British decision makers can be listed as under:

- Lord Clement Attlee, Prime Minister of Great Britain from August 1945 to 1950. Along with him were Lord Pethick-Lawrence (Secretary of State for India and Burma) and Sir Stafford Cripps (President of the Board of Trade) in London.

- The Viceroy of India, Field Marshal Viscount Lord Wavell (at the time of the INA trials and Naval mutiny)
- The last Viceroy of India, Lord Louis Mountbatten (however, the decision to free India had been taken by the time he was appointed. It was his task to implement that decision and actualise time frames).
- Commander-in-Chief India, General (later, Field Marshal) Claude Auchinleck and his superiors in the Imperial General Staff in London. Communications between them would provide the vital input about the military impact of the INA and subsequent mutinies in the Royal Indian Navy, Air Force and some units of the British Indian Army. This would be the most critical and decisive input.
- The British Governors of the Indian Provinces and their reports to the Viceroy on the internal situation in the wake of the INA trials also provide clear insights in to the decision-making process and the ground situation in various states in the wake of the INA trials and the naval mutiny.
- Another valuable source of information are the reports of the Intelligence Bureau whose primary task was to monitor the internal security situation and threats thereto.

The key and pivotal decision maker, however, remains the British Prime Minister of that era, Lord Clement Attlee. Even the then British Monarch King George was bound to act on his advice. It is here that we have a very interesting input about what Attlee said and felt about the grant of Independence to India and precisely how it came about. Before we get on to that it would be useful to recapitulate in some detail the final events that led to the decision to Free India and Transfer Power.

The Final March of Events

On July 26, 1945, in a significant paradox, as it were, Churchill, the celebrated British war leader, lost the elections at the peak of his fame and power. He had successfully led the British in a six-year-long war. Just when the final triumph came, a war-weary population showed him the door. The British people were physically, emotionally and psychologically drained by that war. As a consequence, they showed their most celebrated and charismatic war leader, Winston Churchill, the door. On July 26, Churchill, conceding defeat in the general elections, advised the King to ask Attlee to form a Government. Early in August 1945, Clement Attlee had taken charge.

The worst person in the Attlee Cabinet, Nehru felt, was Sir Stafford Cripps. Early in 1942, Cripps had brought Indians an offer (the famous Cripps Offer) of Dominion Status at the end of the war and participation in an All-India Government meanwhile. *Subsequent negotiations had failed over defence. The British had insisted that defence remains their responsibility. Cripps had publicly blamed the Congress Party for this failure.*

Now the same Cripps was in Attlee's Cabinet. When Attlee had been officiating PM in the wartime coalition government for a while, he had on August 9, 1942, approved the arrests and proscription of the Congress Party. Thereafter Attlee's remarks had dwelt less on the necessity of bringing independence to the subcontinent than on the difficulty of doing so (Peter W. Fay, *The Forgotten Army*, p. 430). Nehru therefore was most suspicious and sceptical of Attlee. Early indications after the formation of the new Labour Government were not encouraging. In his address to Parliament, George V had promised "to press on with the "development of My Colonial Empire and the welfare of its people." That was the tone and tenor of the Attlee Government when it took charge in 1945. The Labour Party did not have a clear mandate for decisive change. Though the general elections had given it a majority of almost 150 seats in the House of Commons, at the polls it had received only 2 million more votes than the Conservatives. Attlee had won primarily on the basis of his domestic programme. In the realm of Colonial and Foreign Policy, Labour would be more conservative than the Conservatives themselves.

I am recounting this specifically, *to fault the thesis of the Court Historians, that because of the continual non-violent struggle of the Congress over the past several decades, a kind of momentum towards freedom had been built up and what was germane or critical, was simply the process of negotiations, which Gandhi and Nehru seemed to lead.* This is very far from the truth. The Congress Party's last charge, the Quit India Movement of 1942, had unfortunately petered out completely. The British had totally weathered this storm and they felt they were on top of the situation. They were absolutely in no mood to make any concessions/compromises about India's freedom.

On August 13, 1945, Japan had surrendered. The provincial governments declared two to three days of holiday. The most joyous, however, were the Americans and British servicemen, eager to go home. War weariness was the primary sentiment. On August 23, 1945, the Domei News Agency of Japan announced the death of Bose in an air crash. Picked up instantly, it had created a stir right across the subcontinent. Schools closed, markets shut; in Bombay, the cotton mills stopped working; in Ahmedabad, there was a general "Hartal," writes Fay.

Attlee, meanwhile, had selected Pethick-Lawrence as his Secretary of State for India. He was old, amiable and did not rub Indians the wrong way. Lord Wavell was immensely relieved. With the surrender of Japan, normal political life in the subcontinent could not be postponed indefinitely. The sudden surrender of Japan forced the issue by depriving Delhi of the postponement rationale. Hence on August 21, 1945, Wavell had given notice for the Central and Provincial elections, the first since 1937. On August 22, the Congress Party's proscription was ended, to enable it to participate in these elections. The party was in disarray, as it had to now collect its workers and reopen its offices. As I have cited, its top leadership had emerged from prison, virtually broken in spirit and with all fight seemingly knocked out of them. It needed an issue to galvanise itself and the Indian masses. Luckily for the Congress, the ghost of Bose seemed to rekindle the freedom struggle with a major bang. The issue was provided by Bose and his INA. It put life back into a virtually moribund Congress. It was the ghost of Bose who rejuvenated the Congress and the Freedom Struggle. R. F. Mudie, the Home Member of Viceroy's Executive Council had written about Bose, "The Bengali's influence over the INA was substantial. It affects all races, castes and communities. Men admired him for organising India's First 'National Army' and for so conducting himself and that the Japanese were forced to treat Indians as allies. In the eyes of many, he stood on a level with Gandhi."

Nehru had initially opposed the launch of the 1942 Quit India Movement (as had most CWC members). They had virtually been bulldozed by Gandhi into launching this crusade. *The simple fact is that by then the views of Bose and Gandhi had begun to coincide markedly. Gandhi realised, in retrospect, that Bose had been absolutely right. This was India's last and desperate chance to attain freedom. It was now or never. It was "Do or Die." The Congress Party had thereafter launched its final non-violent crusade.* The British had used unabashed violence to crush this popular uprising. To avoid any chances of peaceful agitations, they had used five divisions or *some 57 Battalions of white troops.* That had crushed the Quit India Movement. This last charge had left the Mahatma psychologically exhausted and spent. He almost died in prison. This was perhaps when the British worked on Nehru in prison. When they released him, they were sure he was going to be reasonable. After all, he had initially opposed the launch of the Quit India Movement during the war and he had threatened to march against Bose if he invaded India along with the Japanese. He was perhaps the most anglicised of all Indian leaders.

Out of jail, Nehru and *the Congress were soon pushed by the rising tide of anger and angst over the death of Netaji and the trials of the INA. A storm was rising all over India and the Congress leaders including Nehru were simply lifted by this rising tide of resentment and anger.* The return of the INA prisoners had started in July 1945 itself. After the war ended, this process was speeded up. The British were making a serious mistake. In hindsight, they may have decided to leave them in Burma and Malaya. But they brought them back in shiploads to Chittagong and Calcutta. From here they were sent to camps in Jhingugacha and Nilganj (near Calcutta), to Kirkee (outside Pune) and Bahadurgarh (close to Delhi), to Attock and Multan in the Punjab (now in Pakistan). At Bahadurgarh, the men of the Indische Legion were brought in. "Blacks" and those required to depose against them were concentrated in the Red Fort in Delhi.

By early September 1945, some 7,000 INA men had reached India. By early November, this had risen to 12,000. Some 3,000 had been allowed to rejoin their families. By December 1945, releases were averaging more than 600 a week. The INA men were getting reinjected into the national bloodstream. Stories of their glorious struggles were now proliferating all across the land, along with much embellishment. The INA POW cages were arousing public curiosity and anger. "These thousands, spreading all over the country," said Nehru to Krishna Menon, "will make a difference, perhaps a great difference, for they are hard as nails and very anti-British." Events were building up for a repeat of 1857.

The violence that broke out all over India in the wake of the INA trials was simply unprecedented. In Delhi, in Calcutta, in Mumbai and Karachi the crowds poured out into the streets. Over a lakh of people surged out in Calcutta. Police firing simply failed to stop them. The crowds would stop for a few seconds then simply surge forward again. In all his years the Mahatma had never been able to mobilise such large-scale and extremely agitated mobs. The very scale of the rioting left the British dazed and petrified. The most worrisome was the sullen and ominous mood in the Indian military units. The British were terrified of the storm that was building up in South Asia. Was it heading for another 1857 style mutiny? If so, where were the white British troops to quell such an uprising? At the very least it needed five British Divisions. But most of them had been sent back to England for demobilisation. The American and British troops were homesick and simply war weary. They were in no mood to attempt a second re-conquest of India, this time in the face of 25 lakh combat hardened Indian soldiers who had done so well in the war and were right then being demobilised.

Unprecedentedly, the INA trials were very public, to strike terror into the hearts of the armed forces. Due to the sympathy toward Netaji and the INA in general, there was an instant and large outpouring of passion and patriotism in Indians. It was almost like an explosion. These stories were being shared via wireless sets and through media in general on the ships, where the sailors who were discriminated against got inspired to revolt. The British claimed that the causes for the subsequent Naval mutiny were entirely local and Hygiene factors based, i.e., the bad quality of food, the thinness of the dal and bad accommodation, etc. That however was just the tip of the iceberg of anger and humiliation at racial slurs that had accumulated over the years. Just as the greased cartridges were not the actual but merely the precipitating causes of the 1857 uprising, food, etc., seemed to be the triggering cause of the 1946 revolt. But it had been brewing for long and could be clearly traced back to the intense resentment born of the INA trials.

Royal Indian Navy Revolt

The INA trials had inflamed the Indian soldiers, sailors and airmen of the British Indian Armed Forces. The first to revolt were the sailors of the Royal Indian Navy. It was a massive and widespread rebellion. At its peak some 20,000 sailors on 78 ships and 20 shore establishments had revolted. They had pulled down the Union Jack and hoisted in its stead, the tri-colour Congress Flag. They had refused to obey their British officers, chased them out and manhandled them. They had marched through the streets of Mumbai and Karachi with portraits of Netaji, shouting the INA slogans of "Jai Hind" and "Chalo Dilli." The revolt had occurred first in the Royal Indian Navy, an All India, All-Class Service. It spread next to the Royal Indian Air Force (also all-Indian, all-class based). Mostly it was the signallers who could communicate with diverse units, who spearheaded this agitation. They had spread on wireless the news of the INA trials and generally coordinated the revolt. The British were petrified. This was the spectre that had been haunting them so far, of a dam about to burst.

Auchinleck now warned his Army commanders that they could no longer rely on the soldiers of the Indian Army. He warned the Government in London to hastily announce a date for the British departure. Both the soldiers, Wavell and Auchinleck, were now crystal clear, it was all over for the Raj. The sheet anchor for its continuance, its very centre of gravity, was the loyalty of the Indian sepoy to the Raj. With this in serious doubt, they were clear that it was curtains for the empire. Did they want to go with grace or did they want a very messy and bloody exit? For this time the Congress leaders had been able to bail the British out. They had talked the naval mutineers into surrendering. The key question was, for how long?

Royal Indian Air Force Revolt

Just twelve days before the Indian Naval Mutiny (which started on February 18, 1946), 600 members, including officers of the Royal Indian Air Force (RIAF) camp situated close by on Bombay's Marine Drive, had gone on a hunger strike as a protest against a racial insult by the Camp Commander. The revolt in the Navy soon spread to the ranks of the Royal Indian Air Force. Indian airmen at many airbases went on strike. They too refused to obey their British officers and shouted pro-INA slogans in Karachi and other cities.

Jabalpur Army Mutiny

The last straw that broke the camel's back however was the spread of this armed revolt finally to the Indian Army, the real source of the strength of the Raj in India. On the quiet morning of February 26, 1946, as an aftermath of the naval mutiny, some 120 army men of the "J" company of the Signals Training Centre (STC), Jabalpur, defied their British superiors and broke free from their barracks. Part of a radio-signalling unit, they were sick and tired of the racist abuse heaped on them by their paranoid British counterparts. There was complete commotion for some days.

Meanwhile Lord Pethick-Lawrence made a momentous declaration in the House of Lords on February 19, 1946 (just a day after the start of the naval mutiny) in which he announced the decision of the British government to send a special mission, consisting of himself, Sir Stafford Cripps and A. V. Alexander to resolve the constitutional deadlock in India. This was the beginning of the end, the first nail in the coffin of the empire. Meanwhile British General Staff had begun serious planning to cope with wider mutinies and unrest in the army. Some of the declassified documents of the British Indian Army of that period make chilling reading. Sample these:

> *If, however, the Indian Armed Forces did not remain loyal ... we would be faced with the necessity of providing five British divisions for India, with the consequent abandonment of commitments in other areas hitherto regarded as inescapable, serious effects on our import and export programmes and worldwide repercussions on the release scheme. The only alternative to this would be ignominious withdrawal from the whole of India. Five British divisions incidentally were just not available. Most divisions were being hurriedly shipped back home because the soldiers were desperately homesick.*

The Report by the Chiefs of Staff is an important document that brings to light several important points connected with India's independence. It clearly brings out the fact that the British Government was seriously considering the option of creating Pakistan in June 1946, not because of the lack of agreement with the political parties—this was still being negotiated by the Cabinet Mission—but due to the threat of disaffection in the Indian armed forces. At a point in time it was being considered that all British forces and families would first concentrate in Pakistan and then be shipped/flown out. This option was ruled out only because it did not serve British strategic interests. *The disparity in the outlook of British officials in London and Delhi is also clearly visible; for the former, Britain's long-term strategic interest dictated continuation of British rule, while those closer to the scene of action, such as Wavell and Auchinleck, realised that it was time to go. Had the Indian armed forces remained loyal or had there been enough British divisions to keep them in check, the British would never have left India.*

Early in September 1946 the Viceroy forwarded to London a plan for phased withdrawal from India, which was a revised version of the Breakdown Plan of the Cabinet Mission. This had been rejected by the British Government as it did not help British strategic interests. Wavell could see that the situation was steadily deteriorating, and unless a clear policy was announced, India could slide into anarchy. After consulting the Governors and the C-in-C, he estimated that the British could hold on for not more than 18 months. *The Secretary of State, Lord Pethick-Lawrence, did not agree with Wavell's appreciation. He felt that it was still possible to hold on to India, and proposed further European recruitment to augment British troops in India.* By this time, serious communal riots had broken out in East Bengal and in the Punjab, resulting in sizeable casualties among Hindus as well as Muslims. A new Interim Government headed by Jawaharlal Nehru had been installed at Delhi, with Sardar Baldev Singh as the Defence member. In a letter dated September 12 to Auchinleck, who had recently been appointed a Field Marshal, Nehru discussed the withdrawal of British forces from India; pulling out Indian troops from the Netherlands East Indies and Iraq; and the future of the Indian Army. In a broadcast to the Armed Forces on October 9, Baldev Singh announced the setting up of a committee to accelerate the pace of nationalisation. In view of these developments, Pethick-Lawrence's proposal to raise additional European troops for India appeared surreal.

Refusing to take no for an answer, *Wavell sent a strongly worded note to the Secretary of State on October 23,* in which he reiterated his demand for a firm declaration of the policy of the British Government. His plan, he wrote, was based on two main assumptions:

- The object was to transfer power to India without undue delay and with the minimum of disorder and bloodshed; to secure the interests of the Minorities and to provide for the safety of the 90,000 Europeans in India;
- *The power of the British Government in India was weakening daily, and could not be sustained beyond 18 months. Using exceptionally strong language, Wavell made it clear that as the man on the spot, it was his responsibility to advise the Government of the action to be taken to achieve these objects. "If HMG consider that my advice shows lack of balance and judgment, or that I have lost my nerve, it is of course their duty to inform me of this and to replace me," he wrote. "But they take a very grave responsibility upon themselves if they simply neglect my advice."* Wavell ended by emphasising that they *"must have an emergency plan in readiness; and if it is agreed that we cannot hope to control events for longer than 18 months from now, we shall have to make up our minds and make a definite pronouncement at least in the first half of 1947. While I agree that we should not leave India till we have exhausted every possible means of securing a constitutional settlement, we can make no contribution to a settlement once we have lost all power of control."*

In December 1946 the British Government invited Nehru, Baldev Singh, Jinnah and Liaquat Ali Khan to London for discussions, along with the Viceroy. During his visit, Wavell again pressed for adoption of the Breakdown Plan, urging the Government to announce that they would withdraw all control from India by March 1948. *Some Cabinet Ministers such as Bevin and Alexander, who were imperialists at heart, balked at the prospect of a stark announcement of the ending of the British Raj.* Prime Minister Attlee also felt strongly that the British should not relinquish control until at least a constitutional settlement had been reached. Since the chances of reaching an amicable settlement appeared dismal, Attlee's views seemed illusory. After a series of meetings, the *India and Burma Committee decided to recommend that March 32, 1948 should be announced as the date by which the British would hand over power in India.* Wavell pressed for a firm announcement in this regard by the British Government. Attlee replied to Wavell on December 21, 1946, giving the impression that his proposal had been by and large accepted.

Though the freedom movement had developed considerable momentum by the time the war ended, the assumption that it would have achieved independence on its own would be erroneous. With the vast resources at their disposal, it would not have been difficult for the British authorities in India to muzzle the movement, as they had done in 1930 and 1942. The only reason for them not being able to resort to such measures after 1945 was the uncertain dependability of the Army. Had the Indian soldier remained staunch, or adequate British forces been available, it is most unlikely that freedom would have come in 1947. If nothing else, it would have been delayed by 10 to 15 years.

The redoubtable Lt Gen Sinha, was one of the first Indian officers to be posted at the most prestigious Military Operations (MO) Directorate in Delhi in 1947. This was hitherto manned only by British officers. The outgoing British officer he was taking charge from handed over the keys of the Top Secret documents to him and left in a great hurry, as it were. Therein Gen Sinha saw two Top Secret files meant for British officers only. One was a Contingency Plan to fly in British troops to deal with any mutiny in the Indian armed Forces. This called for flying in some five British divisions to quell such an uprising. The problem really was where were these five divisions? I had learnt this first-hand from Gen Sinha himself, a few months before he passed away.

Operation Gondola

The second was Op Gondola—a plan to evacuate British civil and military personnel from India in the event of a major armed uprising. This gives the clearest insight into the state of mind of the British and the real reason why they left in such a tearing hurry in 1947.

Partition

Lord Louis Mountbatten had taken over from Field Marshal Wavell as India's last Viceroy and later its first Governor General. He had, rather arbitrarily and whimsically, advanced the date of British withdrawal from India from the earlier target date of June 1948 to August 15, 1947 simply because that happened to be the anniversary of his South East Asia Command's Victory over Japan. This led to the holocaust of partition in which over 2 million Indians and Pakistanis were killed and some 14.5 million were uprooted and displaced. It saw the most massive mass migrations in human history. Perhaps the real underlying intention was to seed such chaos that the newly formed Dominions would beg to be reincorporated back into the empire.

The Attlee Testimony

Ranjan Bhora in his eminently researched paper in the Historical Journal of India writes:"Ramesh Chandra Majumdar, the eminent Indian historian who passed away recently, and who by virtue of his challenges to several historical myths can rightly be called the Dean of new historians in India, observed in his book, *Three Phases of India's Struggle for Freedom*:

> 'There is, however, no basis for the claim that the Civil Disobedience Movement directly led to independence. The campaigns of Gandhi ... came to an ignoble end about fourteen years before India achieved independence ... During the First World War the Indian revolutionaries sought to take advantage of German help in the shape of war materials to free the country by armed

revolt. But the attempt did not succeed. During the Second World War, Subhas Bose followed the same method and created the INA. In spite of brilliant planning and initial success, the violent campaigns of Subhas Bose failed ... *The Battles for India's freedom were also being fought against Britain, though indirectly, by Hitler in Europe and Japan in Asia. None of these scored direct success, but few would deny that it was the cumulative effect of all the three that brought freedom to India. In particular, the revelations made by the INA trial, and the reaction it produced in India,* made it quite plain to the British, already exhausted by the war, that they *could no longer depend upon the loyalty of the sepoys for maintaining their authority in India.* This had probably the greatest influence upon their final decision to quit India.'"

Bhora continues: "apart from revisionist historians, it was none other than Lord Clement Attlee himself, the British Prime Minster responsible for conceding independence to India, who gave a shattering blow to the myth sought to be perpetuated by court historians, that Gandhi and his movement had led the country to freedom. Chief Justice P.B. Chakraborty of Calcutta High Court, who had also served as the acting Governor of West Bengal in India, disclosed the following in a letter addressed to the publisher of Dr. R.C. Majumdar's book, *A History of Bengal.* The Chief Justice wrote:

"You have fulfilled a noble task by persuading Dr. Majumdar to write this history of Bengal and publishing it ... In the preface of the book Dr. Majumdar has written that he could not accept the thesis that Indian independence was brought about solely, or predominantly by the non-violent civil disobedience movement of Gandhi.

"When I was the acting Governor, Lord Attlee, who had given us independence by withdrawing the British rule from India, spent two days in the Governor's palace at Calcutta during his tour of India. At that time I had a prolonged discussion with him regarding the real factors that had led the British to quit India. My direct question to him was that since Gandhi's 'Quit India' movement had tapered off quite some time ago and in 1947 no such new compelling situation had arisen that would necessitate a hasty British departure, why did they have to leave?

"In his reply Attlee cited several reasons, *the principal among them being the erosion of loyalty to the British Crown among the Indian Army and Navy personnel as a result of the military activities of Netaji. Toward the end of our discussion I asked Attlee what was the extent of Gandhi's influence upon the British decision to quit India. Hearing this question, Attlee's lips became twisted in a sarcastic smile as he slowly chewed out the word, 'm-i-n-i-m-a-l!'"* [46]

Bhora concludes: "When the new version of the history of the Twentieth Century India, and especially the episode of the country's unique struggle for independence comes to be written, it will no doubt single out but one person who made the most significant and outstanding contribution among all his compatriots toward the emancipation of his motherland from the shackles of an alien bondage. During World War II this man strode across two continents like a colossus, and the footsteps of his army of liberation reverberated through the forests and plains of Europe and the jungles and mountains of Asia. His armed assaults shook the very foundations of the British Empire.

His name was Subhas Chandra Bose."

This assesment is echoed by Dr Balashib Ambedkar, the framer of India's Constitution and its first Law Minister. Babasaheb would not have been surprised with Sir Attlee's admission, for he had foreseen it. He told the BBC in 1955 that from his "own analysis" he had concluded that "two things led the Labour party to take this decision" [to free India]. Ambedkar continued: "The national army that was raised by Subhas Chandra Bose. The British had been ruling the country in the firm belief that whatever may happen in the country or whatever the politicians do, they will never be able to change the loyalty of soldiers. That was one prop on which they were carrying on the administration. And that was completely dashed to pieces. They found that soldiers could be seduced to form a party—a battalion to blow off the British."

Bohra writes: "*This 'unimpeachable' truth will come as a shock to most Indians brought up to believe that the Congress movement driven by the 'spiritual force' of Mahatma Gandhi forced the British to leave India. But both the evidence and the logic of history are against this beautiful but childish fantasy; it was the fear of mutiny by the Indian armed forces—and not any 'spiritual force'—that forced the issue of freedom.* The British saw that the sooner they left India the better for themselves, for, at the end of the war, India had some three million men under arms."

Majumdar had reached the same conclusion years ago.

5

Conclusive Evidence: The Commander-in-Chief Gen (Later Fd Mshl) Claude Auchinleck's Reports to The Viceroy

If one is to accurately gauge the impact of the INA uprising and trials upon the thinking and repercussions on the actions of the British in India, the most crucial and critical inputs would perforce come from the reports sent by the C-in C the British Indian Army to the Viceroy and also to the Imperial General Staff in London. The most critical and important of them all is the Military Appreciation of the Situation in India in the wake of the INA trials that was written in end November 1945. It is an emphatic and clear document, that in the cold and precise language of a military appreciation, sums up the prevailing situation and the profound impact of the INA on the continued loyalty and reliability of the Indian troops. It clinically analyses the scenarios that could emerge and then seeks to fashion military response options and the resources that would be needed to implement them. This documentation gives us the clearest insight into the military thinking of that era and highlights for us the enormous psychological impact of the INA .These reports are most reflective of the thinking of the British military in India. As such they provide authentic, primary and first-hand documentary evidence that clearly helps us to identify the impact of the INA on the final

British decision to leave India. Dr Kalyan De has rendered yeoman service in digging out these reports from the British Archives about the transfer of power in India. Because of their very seminal importance I have decided to cite these documents in full rather than just quoting relevant extracts. The reports cited in this chapter have been extracted from *The Transfer of Power*, Vol. 6, pp. 530 and 939. The first is Gen Auchinleck's letter to Fd Mshl Viscount Wavell dated November 24, 1945

(Wavell Papers. Official Correspondence India, January-December 1945, pp. 374-78).

TOP SECRET AND PERSONAL

1. GENERAL AUCHINLECK TO FIELD MARSHAL VISCOUNT WAVELL WAVELL PAPERS. OFFICIAL CORRESPOMDENCE: INDIA, JANUARY-DECEMBER 1945, PP. 374-78

NEW DELHI,
24 NOVEMBER 1945

My dear Lord Wavell,
I have been discussing further the question of the I.N.A. trials as a result of meetings held between the Home Department and certain representatives of Provincial Governments.

2. The representatives of Provinces expressed considerable uneasiness about the political situation which might result from a continuance of the present agitation. They felt that a decision to execute any of the accused in the present trials might result in unrest on a scale more serious than in 1921 and 1942. The Punjab, who were the spokesmen in this matter, and who are of course the Province most deeply affected, suggested at first that *while the present trials*

should be carried through, it should be decided now that there should be no further trials, except for murder and atrocities, and that any sentences of death which are passed by the Court should be commuted. The charges of waging war against the King-Emperor should be dropped in future trials. They attach great importance to a clear restatement of policy and publication of the names of those to be tried. I attach a paper which gives in convenient form the views expressed by the Punjab representative.

3. After discussion with certain officers here, the Provincial representatives agreed that the charge of waging war against the King-Emperor could not be dropped. They recognised that to do this would amount to almost complete condonation of disloyalty. There is also the legal argument that in many cases the charges of brutality and murder would not stand unless that of waging war was also proved. They continued however to think that the trials should be limited to those involving brutality and murder of such a nature that it could not be defended as an act committed in good faith by a combatant.

4. At present the categories to be brought to trial are:

(a) Any person actively instrumental in causing the death of any British or Allied subject, whether in or out of battle.
(b) Any person responsible for the brutal treatment of any British or Allied subject.
(c) Any person taking a responsible part in the capture and handing over to the enemy of any British or Allied subject.
(d) Officers, V.C.O.s, and I.O.R.s who became officers in the I.N.A. and 950 Regiment and took a leading part against us.

(e Fujiwara volunteers. I have discussed the whole question with my civil and military advisers whose views differ widely. One point of view is that no further trials should take place except in cases of brutality which cannot be defended by the practices and laws of any civilised people. Those who hold this view would convene no further trials for offences which would be legally defensible had they been committed by members of the army of a belligerent. In other words, they would exclude persons who killed British or Allied troops in battle, who handed over ordered or carried out what purported to be legal sentences of death in the field. They would, however, still couple with the charge of brutality that of waging war against the King-Emperor, in order to establish the principle that this should not be condoned.

5. The grounds urged by them in support of these views are: Firstly, the present I.N.A. trials are agitating all sections of Indian public opinion deeply and have also provided the Congress with an excellent election cry. The agitation in the country is likely to increase if there are further trials of the type of present trials. Limitation of trials to the categories proposed is likely to allay public excitement and create a better feeling in the country. There can be no legitimate criticism against trials of persons accused of brutal acts which cannot be justified or defended under colour of any law.

Secondly, the proposed course of action is unlikely to undermine the stability or the reliability of the Indian Armed Forces. The principle that treason cannot be condoned will have been vindicated by the continuance of the present trials and the addition of the charge of waging war in the further trials proposed. *With the existing Armed Forces recruited from all parts and all classes of India and modern means of communications and the growth of nationalist feeling in the country, it is quite impossible to isolate the Armed Forces from the rest of the country. There is evidence to show that there is no general resentment in the Indian Army against the I.N.A.* There are reasons to believe that Indian officers of the three Services would, generally speaking, approve the proposed limitation of trials. Trial for tortures committed on Indian prisoners of war in order to force them to join the I.N.A. would satisfy the prisoners of war and their relations. The Indian Armed Forces would also no doubt realise that none except the "whites" would be retained in the Indian Army. On the other hand, further trials of the type now proceeding is likely to create more sympathy for the I.N.A. than is the case at present and "greys" and "blacks" on release would tend to be regarded, to an increasing extent, as martyrs and would be exploited by the Congress and other political parties.

Thirdly, they do not believe that there is much in the argument that the proposed policy would amount to greater condonation of treason than the present policy, for under the latter, *it is proposed to prosecute no more than 75 out of about 17,500 "blacks" and "greys" who are under the law guilty of waging war against the King.*

6. Others of my advisers feel that this would amount to recognising the belligerent status of the I.N.A. and accepting the view that a soldier may change his allegiance because of his political views, or because he can secure better conditions by so doing. They argue that the inclusion of the charge of waging war in cases of brutality would

be no more than a gesture; and in fact by limiting future trials to this small category, we should have admitted that a mistake had been made in bringing to trial the first three officers, in whose cases (with one doubtful exception) it could be argued that the acts with which they are charged were committed in execution of what the accused believed to be their duty. Once the premise is granted that they genuinely considered they were justified in joining the I.N.A. and that it was a belligerent army. Those who hold this view feel that to exclude the trial of those coming in categories (a), (c), (d) and (e) above would undermine the discipline of the Indian Army. They point out that there were some officers of the Indian Army who went over at once to the enemy and who were instrumental in making large numbers of their men follow their lead. One example is an officer who had been placed in command of a particular unit two or three days before the surrender, and who shortly afterwards ordered the unit to join the I.N.A. The loyal men of this regiment are very bitter against this officer; and it is pointed out that those who followed him have forfeited their pay, or part of it, and have been dismissed or discharged from the Army because they obeyed his orders. It is contended that it would be contrary to all our ideas of justice if he were punished no more severely than they. They would not therefore make any change in the present policy.

7. Between these two points of view there is another. It is suggested that we should decide now that although the confirmation of every sentence must be considered on its merits, it should be taken as a general principle that the death sentence would be commuted in cases in which it could be argued that the accused had

been carrying out what he thought to be his duty. As a general rule, however, the death sentence would not be commuted in cases of brutality, which could be excused on no such grounds. On the conclusion of the first trial, the sentence would probably be commuted to one of a short period of imprisonment. My decision would be published with a brief statement to the effect that the trials had been held to vindicate the legal principle, but that since it had been decided that the accused were endeavouring to carry out what they conceived mistakenly to be their duty, it had been decided to reduce the sentence. It would be indicated at the same time that this principle would be followed in any future trials in which the same considerations seemed to prevail. It is argued that this course would take much of the sting from the Nationalist attack, since it would become clear that the sentence of death would be carried out only in cases of brutality, which it is believed that no one will wish to defend. There will be nothing in this course inconsistent in any way with our previous utterances.

8. After very careful consideration I feel that the first course is the wisest. The arguments in its favour have been stated above, and I am left with no doubt that from the point of view of public opinion in general it would be the most satisfactory. From the point of view of the Army, there is undoubtedly a risk; but I believe it should be taken. The evidence reaching us now increasingly goes to show that the general opinion in the Army (as opposed to that of certain units and individuals who have particular reasons for bitterness) is in favour of leniency. If you agree that this first course should be adopted, we would limit future trials to cases of brutality; and in the case of the present trials, the

sentences would be commuted if it was clear from the evidence when the trials are concluded that the accused were carrying out what they believed to be their duty. I have considered whether in that case the sentence should be commuted to one of imprisonment; but on the whole I believe that this would forfeit some of the advantages of the policy and there would be little to be gained by it. If the sentence is to be commuted, it can only be on the grounds that the men acted in good faith: and in that case it would be illogical to imprison them. There would further be the danger that if imprisoned, they would be released on a new Government coming into power and there might then be a temptation to reinstate them in the Army. If they are released now, I consider this would be most unlikely.

9. I enclose for reference a copy of the statement we put out on the 27th August. It will be seen that the only point in the present policy which differs from that then announced is that we did say that we would proceed against "leaders who appeared consciously to have embraced the Japanese or German cause." It is true that at the time we meant by that to include people who would now be discharged; but it seems to me that we are unlikely to be taunted with leaving out these people, and if we are, it does not very much matter.

10. I attach a draft Press Communique which sets out the first view. It has been argued that this does not make it clear that the policy has been changed and that therefore it may attract little attention; but I think that while to the general reader this Communique will not give the impression of a change of policy, it will be read carefully by the leaders, to whom also the

implications will be pointed out unofficially, and that the latter, who have already shown signs of feeling that they have gone too far, will be glad to meet us on this and reduce the agitation. It is unfortunate that it is not possible to publish the names of those who will be tried, because the investigations are not yet complete. We have, however, gone as far as is possible in this direction at present.

11. I should therefore be glad to know whether Your Excellency approves of my taking this line. If so, it will be necessary to inform the Secretary of State of what we are doing, since there has been a considerable modification of our views since we first told him that we should be proceeding to try by Court Martial some 600 people.

12. The Home Department were of course represented in the discussions with Provincial Governments, but the Hon'ble Home Member has not yet had an opportunity of discussing with me the policy I now suggest, nor has he seen the Press Communique.

Yours sincerely,
C. J. AUCHINLECK

Enclosure

PUNJAB GOVERNMENT

His Excellency (the Governor of the Punjab) discussed this case on 15th November 1945 with C.S. and D.I.G. and decided that the following proposals should be made at the conference at Delhi:

1. The trials of Shah Nawaz, Sehgal and Dhillon cannot be stopped now as this would betray

weakness and a lack of courage, which Congress would immediately exploit and which would make successful Government impossible.
2. The crux of the matter is whether Government intend to stand firm in the event of the death sentences being imposed. *If Government intend to carry out the death sentences, they must be prepared to face unparalleled agitation, more widespread than in 1919 and 1942, and to use ruthless force to suppress it.*
Another "fast unto death" by Gandhi as a protest must also be taken into consideration. The agitation which would follow the execution of these three men and the force which would have to be used to suppress it would prejudice any hope of a settlement with India.

3. In these circumstances, the only practical solution would appear to be to *carry on the trials and for the Commander-in-Chief to commute the death sentences if imposed. Their commutation should be announced simultaneously with the announcement of the death sentences themselves. There should be no time-lag in which to work up violent agitation.*

4. Future trials should be confined to charges of murder and atrocities. Charges of treason and waging war against the King should be dropped. Publicity should be given to this decision now.

5. *Publicity should also be given to the decision to treat the I.N.A. leniently. The small numbers to be tried should be compared with the large numbers to be released,* and the specific charges on which members of the I.N.A. are to be tried should be stated. The actual numbers of officers and men to be tried should be given.

6. Every attempt should be made to get Britain and America to give publicity to the trials, to feature the atrocities committed by the I.N.A. on their own countrymen, and to publicise the leniency and generosity shown by Government towards the I.N.A. in spite of the fact that its members broke their oath of allegiance and waged war against Allied arms. Publicity should also be given in India, and if possible in the U.S.A., to the courage and steadfastness of those who refused to join the I.N.A., sometimes at the cost of their lives. Such men should be given special treatment. Those who wish to stay in the Army should be encouraged to do so, as they may form a valuable hard core of loyalty.

7. Every effort should be made to speed up the trials as delay will aggravate the internal situation seriously. There is very little hope that the public will attach much importance to the prosecution story or be impressed by the charges of murder and brutal conduct. *The I.N.A. are popular heroes, and the treason charge will only increase their popularity. Popular feeling in favour of the I.N.A. is now blinded by racial, political and sentimental feelings. The defence will concentrate entirely on the "patriotism" of Bose and the I.N.A. and will draw freely on sentiment and racial feeling.* The press will follow its lead. Already its tone is worse than it has ever been before. The result will be that a thoroughly dangerous and explosive situation will be worked up.

8. Seeing that some 20,000 or more members of the I.N.A. are to be released unconditionally, the execution of a mere handful would not have any effect on maintaining discipline in the Army. Where the Army is not ignorant of or apathetic

towards the I.N.A., it is generally sympathetic towards it. There is no active resentment against it, except among the few who suffered at its hands.

(Sd.),–17-11-45
C.M. List of names of those who have so far been selected for trial by Court-Martial.

1. Captain Shah Nawaz, 1/14, Punjab Regiment.
Captain P. K. Sehgal, 2/10, Baluch Regiment.
Lieut. Gurbaksh Singh Dhillon, 1/14 Punjab Regiment.
2. Captain Burhan-ud-Din, 2/10, Baluch Regiment.
3. Subedar Shingara Singh, 5/14, Punjab Regiment.
Jemadar Fateh Khan, 5/14, Punjab Regiment.
4. Captain Abdul Rashid, 1/14, Punjab Regiment.

STRICTLY PERSONAL AND SECRET

II. GENERAL AUCHINLECK TO FIELD MARSHAL VISCOUNT WAVELL WAVELL PAPERS. OFFICIAL CORRESPOMDENCE: INDIA, JANUARY 1946-MARCH 1947, PP. 60-67

13 FEBRUARY 1946

I enclose a copy of a Secret and Personal letter I have addressed to all my G.Os. C.-in-C. Commands, District and Area Commanders and all Commanders of Indian Divisions, in an ex-India, on the subject of the "I.N.A." trials.

Enclosure

STRICTLY PERSONAL AND SECRET NOT TO BE PASSED THROUGH ANY OFFICE

General Auchinleck to Army Commanders -

NEW DELHI,
12 FEBRUARY 1946

I have now been able to study a large number of reports from higher and unit commanders and other sources on the effect of the action taken in respect of the first "I.N.A." trial on the Indian Army as a whole.

It is most important that we should study and analyse carefully these effects, as they may influence very greatly our ability to maintain the solidarity and reliability of the Indian Army in the difficult times which undoubtedly lie ahead of us. It is for this reason that I am writing this letter to you. I have considered the desirability of making a personal public statement in explanation of my action in commuting the sentences of transportation passed by the Court on the first three accused, but I have decided that this would not be in the best interests of discipline or the maintenance of my influence and authority as Commander-in-Chief.

I feel, however, that we should do all we can to remove the feelings of doubt, resentment and even disgust which appear to exist in the minds of quite a number of British officers, who have not the knowledge or the imagination to be able to view the situation as a whole, or to understand the present state of feeling in India.

2. As I see it, the commutation of the sentences of transportation of Shah Nawaz, Dhillon and

Sehgal has had the following effects in India:
(a) On the general public, moderate as well as extremist, Muslim as well as Hindu.
Pleasure and intense relief born of the conviction that *confirmation of the sentences would have resulted in violent internal conflict.*
This feeling does not, in my opinion, spring universally from the idea that the convicted officers were trying to rid India of the British and, therefore, to be applauded, whatever crimes they might commit, but *from a generally genuine feeling that they were patriots and nationalists and that, therefore, even if they were misled they should be treated with clemency, as true sons of India.* In this connection, it should be remembered, I think, that *every Indian worthy of the name is today a "Nationalist," though this does not mean that he is necessarily "anti-British."* All the same, where India and her independence are concerned, there are no "pro-British" Indians.
Every Indian Commissioned Officer is a Nationalist and rightly so, provided he hopes to attain independence for India by constitutional means.

(b) On the Indian officers of the Indian Army.
Except for a few recovered prisoners of war who have suffered much at the hands of their fellow countrymen who joined the so-called "I.N.A.," the vast majority, almost without exception, however much they may like and respect the British, are glad and relieved because of the result of the trial. Most of them admit the gravity of the offence and do not condone it, but practically all are sure that *any attempt to enforce the sentence would have led to chaos in the country at large and probably to mutiny and dissension in the Army culminating in its dissolution, probably on communal lines.*

The more senior and intelligent undoubtedly realise the implications of our having established in principle the seriousness of the crime of forsaking one's allegiance and the wisdom of meeting it with a heavy punishment such as "Cashiering" which carries with it the stigma of disgrace.

They realise that if their future is to be at all secure, discipline and loyalty must be maintained, but they, too, are Nationalists and their feelings are much the same as those of the public at large.

(c) On the V.C.Os, and rank and file of the Indian Army.

In very many units apparently little interest was displayed in the "I.N.A." trials, especially in the more illiterate and educationally backward arms of the Service, such as the infantry and artillery.

In the technical units and amongst clerks, etc., however, interest was keen and widespread.

Some of the V.C.Os, and rank and file had suffered like their officers at the hands of their former comrades who joined the "I.N.A." and perhaps feel correspondingly bitter and disgusted at the leniency shown. This is inevitable and cannot be helped, regrettable though it may be. This section of opinion is relatively small.

The great majority are, I think, pleased that leniency has been shown for a variety of reasons. Many of them have relations and friends from the same villages amongst the "I.N.A." Many think that, as the war is over, bygones should be bygones and a fresh start made.

Others are genuinely nationalistic in outlook and have been affected by agitation and propaganda. *The great majority feel, I think, that the whole episode is unpleasant and discreditable to them as a class and to the Army as a whole, and would wish it forgotten and decently buried as soon as possible.*

Under all this, there is, I think, an uneasy feeling as to the future and doubt as to whether their interests will be as well watched in the days to come as they have been in the past.

(d) On the British officers of the Indian Army.

As I hope already said, the effect on many British officers has been bad, and has led to public criticism which has not been in accordance with the traditional loyalty I am entitled to expect. To these officers, perhaps not always very perceptive or imaginative, an officer is an officer, whether he be Indian or British, and they make no allowance for birth or political aspirations or upbringing, nor do they begin to realise the great political stresses and strains now affecting this country. They are unable to differentiate between the British and Indian points of view.

Moreover, *they forget, if they ever knew, the great bitterness bred in the minds of many Indian officers in the early days of "Indianisation" by the discrimination, often very real, exercised against them, and the discourteous, contemptuous treatment meted out to them by many British officers* who should have known better.

These facts constitute the background against which the decisions should be judged, always keeping before one the object, which is to preserve by all possible means in our power the solidarity of the Indian Army, and of the R.I.N. and the R.I.A.F. as well.

I have not specifically mentioned the two younger services, but everything I have said in this letter applies to them just as much as to the

Army, and perhaps more so, as the ratings or other ranks of these services are better educated and perhaps more politically minded than those of the Army.

3. I would like you also to consider and to impress on others, especially those British officers who have been upset by the result of the first "I.N.A." trial, the effect of the capitulation of Singapore on the Indian troops involved in it, from amongst whom the "I.N.A." was subsequently formed.
Those who have served for many years with Indian troops, as I have done, have always recognised that *the loyalty of our men was really to the officers of the regiment or unit, and that although there may have been some abstract sentiments of loyalty and patriotism to the Government and to the King, the men's allegiance for all practical purposes was focused on the regiment, and particularly on the regimental officers, on whom they depended for the[ir] welfare, advancement and future prospects.*
In these officers their faith and trust was almost childlike, as events have proved time and time again. It is true to say that in almost *every case of serious discontent or indiscipline*, and there have been remarkably few of them, which has occurred in the past fifty years, *the cause could be traced to indifferent officers and bad man-management*.

4. The terrible tragedy of Singapore following on the fall of Hong Kong must have seemed to the great majority of the V.C.Os and rank and file to be the end of all things, and certainly of the British "'Raj" to whom the Army had been used for so many years of war and peace to look to as its universal provider and protector, acting through their own regimental officers.

Their British officers were at once taken from them and they were at once assailed by traitors who had been kept in readiness by the Japanese to seduce them from their allegiance. Their Indian officers in many instances proved false to their trust and used their influence to suborn their own men, skilfully aided and encouraged by the Japanese.

The strain and pressure to which these men, the majority of whom were simple peasant farmers with no cultural or educational background, were subjected is very difficult for any British officer, however experienced, to visualise. Nevertheless it is quite impossible for any British officer to judge them fairly unless he does try to visualise it and realise what these men must have thought and felt.

It is quite wrong to adopt the attitude that because these men had taken service in a British controlled Indian Army that therefore their loyalties must be the same as those of British soldiers. As I have tried to explain, *they had no real loyalty or patriotism towards Britain as Britain, not as we understand loyalty.*

5. So much for the rank and file. The officers who went over present a much more difficult problem. Owing to their presumably superior education, knowledge of the world and experience generally, it is not possible to apply the same reasoning to them, except possibly to the very junior and to those who had been promoted from the ranks, whose background was more limited and whose knowledge was less.

There is no excuse for the regular officers who went over, beyond the fact that *the early stages of "Indianisation" from its inception to the beginning of the late war were badly mismanaged by the British Government of India, and this prepared the ground for disloyalty when the opportunity came.*

There is little doubt that "Indianisation" was at its inception looked on as a political expedient which was bound to fail militarily. There is no doubt also that many senior British officers believed and even hoped that it would fail.
The policy of segregation of Indian officers into separate units, the differential treatment in respect of pay and terms of service as compared with the British officer, and *the prejudice and lack of manners of some—by no means all—British officers and their wives, all went to produce a very deep and bitter feeling of racial discrimination in the minds of the most intelligent and progressive of the Indian officers, who were naturally nationalists, keen to see India standing on her own legs and not to be ruled from Whitehall for ever.*
It is no use shutting one's eyes to the fact that *any Indian officer worth his salt is a Nationalist,* though this does not mean, as I have said before, that he is necessarily anti-British. *If he is anti-British this is as often as not due to his faulty handling and treatment by his British officer comrades.* It is essential for the preservation of future unity that this fact should be fully understood by all British officers.
No Indian officer must be regarded as suspect and disloyal merely because he is what is called a "Nationalist," or in other words, a good Indian!

6. This aspect of the business, though it cannot excuse the action of those officers in going over to the enemy, must be considered as it does provide the background against which we must view the present and the future. Long time before they finally succumbed to circumstances and the persuasion of the Japanese and their extremist

fellow-countrymen. Many of them having joined the first so-called "I.N.A." under Mohan Singh refused to join the second under Bose and spent the next three years as prisoners of war in the islands of the Pacific. This does not excuse their original lapse but does show that they were subjected to conflicting stresses and strains mentally.

7. There remains the matter of the decision to commute the sentences of the first three officers (Sehgal, Dhillon and Shah Nawaz) from "Transportation" to "Cashiering." If, as we have admitted, they were guilty of the worst crime a soldier can commit, then it may well be asked "why be lenient with them?"

In taking the decision to show clemency, the whole circumstances past, present and future had to be considered and was (were] so considered most carefully and over a long period.

The overriding object is to maintain the stability, reliability and efficiency of the Indian Army so that it may remain in the future a trustworthy weapon for use in the defence of India and, we hope, of the Commonwealth as a whole.

It was essential to establish the principle that falseness to his allegiance is a crime which cannot be countenanced in any officer under whatever Government he may be serving. By confirming the finding of the Court and the sentence of "Cashiering" which carries with it the highest degree of disgrace to an officer, we have done this. To have added imprisonment to this sentence would not in any way have helped to emphasise the principle we were concerned to preserve.

On the other hand, having considered all the evidence and appreciated to the best of my ability the general trend of Indian public opinion and of the feeling in the Indian Army, I have no doubt at all that *to have confirmed the sentence of imprisonment solely on the charge of "waging war against the 'King'" would have had disastrous results, in that it would have probably precipitated a violent outbreak throughout the country, and have created active and widespread disaffection in the Army, especially amongst the Indian officers and the more highly educated rank and file.* To have taken this risk would have been seriously to jeopardise our object.

Always keeping before one the difference in outlook between British and Indian, which I have tried to explain in this letter, I decided, therefore, that, in the interests of the future of both India and Britain and because of the unprecedented circumstances of the case, the only proper course to pursue was to confirm the finding and so establish the principle but to show clemency in respect of the sentence. Some bewilderment has been caused, I believe, by the fact that Shah Nawaz who was found guilty of abetment of murder" as well as of "waging war" received the same treatment as the other two accused who were found guilty of "waging war" only. Shah Nawaz's offence, which was committed by him as an officer of the "I.N.A." in the alleged execution of his duty, in that he ordered a sentence authorised by a higher I.N.A. authority to be carried out, did, in the circumstances, flow from his basic offence of "waging war" as a member of the I.N.A. The punishment for this—the principal offence—was "Cashiering" in the case of all three officers. Shah Nawaz did not himself commit any brutal or violent act against any person, but passed on the orders of a superior authority which he claims to have believed to have been properly constituted. It is necessary also to remember that some 20,000 officers and men joined the so-called "I.N.A." and that, even if it were desirable, it would have been a physical impossibility to bring all these men to trial within anything approaching a reasonable period of time.

8. The situation now is that *the principle that the forsaking of his allegiance by a soldier is a crime in any circumstances has been established, and that no further trials on this account alone will be held.* Those against whom there is adequate evidence of murder and brutality will be tried and punished in the ordinary way.
In the second, third and fourth trials the charge of "waging war" has been included in addition to the other charges because these trials were commenced before the finding of the Court in the first trial was known. If the accused in these three trials are found guilty on this charge the Court will pass the sentence of "Transportation for Life" which is the minimum admissible under the Army Act for the offence of "waging war."
When it comes to confirmation of the sentence, however, the facts in respect of the other charges of brutality will be the guiding factor.
In any subsequent trials, the charge of "waging war" will be omitted as our object is now to punish those who may have been guilty of brutal acts towards their former comrades.

9. As to the great mass of rank and file of the so-called "I.N.A.," these are now being examined by Courts of Inquiry as rapidly as possible with a view to finding out whether they are to be classified as "White," "Grey or "Black." I realise very well and so does everyone else at G.H.Q. and in the War Department, the urgent need for disposing of these men at the earliest possible moment, so that the whole affair may have a reasonable chance of being forgotten, which is I am sure the ardent desire of the Army as a whole. At the same time, it is quite certain from

the evidence at our disposal that if this enquiry is not carried out with reasonable thoroughness, great injustice may be done to innocent men. *The temptation, therefore, to_discharge or dismiss all and sundry summarily and without more ado must be resisted.*

10. There is one other criticism which is often made. It is said that we ought to have dealt with the accused summarily in forward areas; that if the men were to be brought to India we should have avoided publicity, and in particular trial in the Red Fort; and that we ought to have put our counter-publicity from the start. *The answer to the first point is that we had to deal with 45,000 men,* in one instance a whole I.N.A. division surrendering without firing a shot.

It was obviously impracticable for forward areas to deal with men on this scale summarily and it was the obvious course to send them back to India where the records and Intelligence organisation existed for interrogation.

As to publicity, I am sure it was right to decide not to hold trials in secret because it would have been thought that the men were not getting a fair trial. Once it was decided that the trials could not be held in secret, it would have been wrong to tuck them away somewhere where defence counsel, relations, etc., could not conveniently attend; and the Red Fort was the most convenient place from nearly every point of view. *We avoided counter-publicity because it was practically certain that a big publicity drive would be represented as prejudicing the accused in their trial; but in any event it is not possible for us to force papers to publish anything which they regard as propaganda and with which they do not agree. We have no control over them in this respect.*

11. This letter has become very lengthy, but I make no apology for this as I consider it essential that the full facts of this sad business should be put before you, so that you in your turn can put them before the officers serving under you, as and when it appears necessary to you.
You should not, in explaining the matter to your officers, quote me as Commander-in-Chief but should use the material I have tried to give you in this letter in any way you think suitable to the purpose as if it came from yourself.

12. Finally let me again state the object: it is to maintain the reliability, stability and efficiency of the Indian Army for the future, whatever Government may be set up in India.
This can be done only if the British and Indian officers of that Army trust and respect each other and continue to work wholeheartedly together for the common cause as they have done in war. It is your task to do your utmost to bring this about and I am sure you will: you have excellent material on which to work.

13. If you are still in doubt on any point or have any suggestions to make in furtherance of our common object, I will be glad if you will let me or the Adjutant General know.

C. J. AUCHINLECK,
General.

Comments
These two letters pertain to the period immediately before and after the INA Trials at the Red Fort and give a very clear idea of the level of apprehension and trepidation that existed in the minds of the British senior officers about the severe repercussions which these trials could have. I have italicised the relevant portions. Fd Mshl Auchinleck clearly acknowledged that the British had invited this disloyalty by their very unfair and racial treatment to all Indian Officers. These racial slurs of the British officers and ladies towards the Indian officers had badly vitiated race relations in the army and other services. The more educated the Indian officers and men, the more keenly were these slurs felt. Every Indian Officer he stated flatly is now a nationalist. Any attempt to execute the INA under-trials would have had serious internal security ramifications.

Much to the chagrin of the Junior British officers, the C-in-C commuted the sentences of all three officers of the INA. The Army Chief in India was armed with adequate intelligence to know the consequences and repercussions of such hasty and foolish acts in such volatile times.

Commander-in-Chief's Military Appreciation of Internal Security Situation in India Fd Mshl Auchinleck's Report to the Chiefs of Staff Committee is the most critical and conclusive piece of evidence in this whole debate. It provides first-hand documentary evidence about the estimate of the British High Command about the post INA trial scenario in a most objective and clinical manner of a military appreciation of the situation. It clearly spells out what is likely to happen and objectively discusses the resources and means to deal with such an emergent situation. One can see the sea change that the INA trials have wrought upon the internal security scenario in such a short time frame. It is vital and crucial for understanding the state of mind and siege mentality that had set into the minds of the British High Command in India. It is a military appreciation of the Internal Security situation by the Commander-in-Chief as of November 24, 1945.They were distinctly unnerved by the ferocity of the riots and agitations that broke out in all towns of India immediately in the wake of the INA trials. The British were absolutely stunned by these and moreover the rising hostility and sullenness of the Indian troops in the wake of this uprising was a cause for alarm and virtual panic. They could simply not count on the continued reliability of Indian troops if called upon to act against their own citizens. This report gives a crystal clear indication of those rising levels of panic in the British military high command in India. This report in fact gives details of worst-case scenarios and contingency planning including for evacuation of British personnel and their families in case of breakout of large-scale mutinies and unrest in Indian Units. British units and families were to concentrate near airports for ease of evacuation by air. Exact number of aircraft needed for operations were computed. This is no expression of opinion. This is an exact and empirical document about the scale and intensity of impact post the INA trials.

They were expecting serious signs of unrest as early as in February 1946 and these estimates turned out to be fairly accurate given the Naval mutiny that followed. It is noteworthy that the senior political leadership in London still hoped to be able to hang on to their empire in India but the military men on the spot—both Auchinleck and Wavell were clear that they had little hope of doing so and that they had at best 18 months to quit with grace. Both these men were not novices, they were old and seasoned India hands.

The appreciation clearly states: "that *in case the Indian armed forces as a whole cease to be reliable, the British Armed forces now available would not be able to control the internal situation or to protect essential communications, nor would any piecemeal reinforcement of these forces be of much avail.*

"To regain control of the situation and to restore essential communications within the country, nothing short of an organised campaign for the reconquest of India is likely to suffice."

The appreciation concludes flatly: *We must be prepared to deal with well organised revolution next Spring, and the possibility of a serious, but less well organised rising at any time during the coming winter.* Such was the impact of the INA trials. It is essential to read this report in full to get a true feel of those times and the panic that was sweeping the British military high command. The report is produced verbatim on the following pages and is a most invaluable document for study and analysis by historians. This is the single most credible and authentic piece of evidence of the impact of the INA of Bose on the British decision to finally quit and depart in a tearing hurry after their major victory in the Second World War. This is a clinching document and primary evidence to settle that historical debate forever.

The appreciation is followed by responses from the Chiefs of Staff Committee in London and replies thereto. This documentation is most vital and clinching evidence. The appreciation of the Commander-in-Chief India provides empirical evidence of the great psychological impact of the INA trials and the unrest within and outside the British Indian Army as a direct consequence of these trials. The Military appreciation leaves nothing to the imagination and candidly highlights the fact that Indian Soldiers can no longer be relied upon to act against their own countrymen and should that happen, the British troops then available in India would be wholly inadequate to control the situation. Even piecemeal reinforcements of White troops would be of no avail. It would virtually need five British divisions to mount a campaign for the re-conquest of India. So dire was the situation perceived to be. The simple fact was that the British troops were desperately homesick and just anxious to get back home. They were in no mood to fight 2.5 million armed Indian soldiers who had just seen extensive combat in the war in almost every theatre. Those five British divisions were just NOT available.

COMMANDER-IN-CHIEF GENERAL AUCHINLECK'S REPORTS TO CHIEFS OF STAFF COMMITTEE AND THEIR REPORTS

The reports are given here as they appeared in "Transfer of Power," Volume 6, pages 576, 638, 673, 675, 975.

I. CHIEFS OF STAFF COMMITTEE

INTERNAL SITUATION IN INDIA APPRECIATION BY COMMANDER-IN-CHIEF,

DATED 24 NOVEMBER 1945

1 DECEMBER 1945

Political Situation

1. Communal trouble is possible any time before during or after the elections. It seems more than likely that there may be serious communal strife between Hindus and Musalmans as a result of the elections.

Anti-Government disorder on a large scale is unlikely until after the elections, that is before April, since this would not be in the interests of Congress. Moreover, most of the political leaders and big businessmen seem at present to be opposed to violent methods.
It is possible that Congress may excite popular feeling over some issue such as that of the I.N.A. to such an extent that they may lose control. On the other hand, their most recent utterances might be held to show that they realise this danger.

Congress methods may, however, force Government to take action, such as the arrest of leaders, *which might precipitate widespread disorder.* In either event it is doubtful if Congress preparations to stage effective widespread disturbance are sufficiently advanced at present though they will undoubtedly steadily improve as time goes on, if the present violent agitation continues. After elections Congress may take part in the constitution making assembly which would give a breathing space of unpredictable length, or they may demand transference of power and proceed to direct action if refused. If Congress intend to take direct action in any event we must assume that they will between now and April perfect plans for widespread simultaneous anti-Government action.

2. It is a reasonable assumption, therefore, that *widespread trouble either communal or anti-government or both is to be expected in the late Spring and may occur before then, but if so will be less organised, and therefore less serious.*

Scale of Disturbances

3. The following factors must be taken into account in assessing the scale and form of widespread and organised disturbance.

(a) Congress will have *learned from the 1942 disturbances how easily rail, road and telephone communications can be disrupted and the paralysing effect of such disruption, particularly on the rapid reinforcement of civil forces in outlying areas;* they will also have realised the error they made in not stirring up the rural population simultaneously with their attacks on communications.

(b) *There are now large quantities of unlicensed arms throughout India and there will be many ex I.N.A. men to use them,* if they feel so inclined. There *will also be a considerable number of ordinary demobilised soldiers in towns and villages, many of whom may be persuaded to support Congress. All these men are trained in the use of weapons, and members of the I.N.A. have some training in the technique of anti-British leadership.*

4. It can be concluded, therefore, that *if and when trouble comes it may be on a greater scale than in August 1942, and is likely to be a combination of the wrecking of communications and widespread disorder in the rural districts.*_

Also *there will be more arms and more men trained in their use at the disposal of the forces of disorder, and the disruption of communications is likely to be designed to isolate and gain control of large tracts.*_

The principal *danger areas are likely to lie in the United Provinces, Bihar and Bengal,* but *trouble must also be expected*
in the Punjab, the Central Provinces and Bombay, but is less likely perhaps in Madras.

Effect of Political Situation on the Armed Forces

5. At the moment the Indian Armed Forces are capable of dealing with either communal or anti-Government disturbances and failures on their part to perform their duty would probably be few and isolated.

6. *It is difficult to assess what the state of the Armed Forces will be in April.* The following factors must be taken into account in assessing

the state of the Indian Armed Forces, other than Gurkha units, which are dealt with separately:

(a) The Congress I.N.A. campaign has undoubtedly taken a strong hold of the country as a whole and must have an *unsettling effect on the Armed Forces* generally and make them receptive to Congress doctrine.

(b) Congress may intensify the present campaign against the use of Indian troops in N.E.I. and F.I.C. and thus attempt to suborn the Army.

This campaign might in the long run have even more dangerous effects than the I.N.A. campaign as it will be based on the accusation that the troops are mere mercenaries.

(c) The general failure in the Armed Forces to understand the inaction on the part of Government against agitators and their doubts as to what might happen under a Congress Government to those now serving.

(d) *As is to be expected, most Indian officers are Nationalists and may, therefore, be over persuaded by Congress propaganda. A large number of British officers whom the rank and file know and respect are likely to be demobilised in the next few months and will be replaced by young and inexperienced officers unknown to the men.*

(e) *The release into recruiting areas of large numbers of potentially disaffected men from the I.N.A. with its possible contaminating effect on individual service men through their families, and on the armed forces as a whole through new recruits, or men returning from leave.*
The great expansion of the armed forces which

has resulted in the creation of a large number of technical and administrative units containing a big proportion of politically conscious and better educated men, and the existence throughout the Army of a great many war promoted and inexperienced V.C.Os and N.C.Os.
These conditions make it more difficult either to discover attempts at political subversion or to take steps to counter them.

(g) The possibility of communal strife occurring within the Armed Forces as a result of political propaganda.

Gurkhas

7. Gurkhas must be considered separately.

Although some joined the I.N.A. most of the factors enumerated in the preceding paragraph are not applicable in their case, particularly (a) (b) (d) (e) and (g), except insofar as the shortage of British E.C.Os may effect their efficiency.
Congress may achieve some success under (a) but (c) is important. Lack of action by Government is almost as important in respect of Gurkhas as it is with any other class, but is likely to affect their efficiency more than their reliability. It is, however, most undesirable that we should differentiate between Gurkhas and other troops of the Indian Army, so far as their supposed reliability for internal defence is concerned, unless and until Indian troops have openly failed in their allegiance.

Conclusion on State of Armed Forces

8. Most of the factors in para. 6 have been in operation for a short time only, or have not yet

begun to operate. It is difficult, therefore, to forecast what effect they may have by next Spring. It is, however, clear that although the morale of the Armed Forces does not appear to be greatly affected yet, the factors mentioned in paragraph 6 are likely steadily to undermine it, while simultaneously Congress preparedness and efficiency will increase.

These processes could produce a very difficult situation by the Spring. That we are alive to the danger is some safeguard, but I consider that ***there must be doubt as to the continued loyalty of the Armed Forces unless Government produce a strong and unequivocal statement of policy comprehensible by the rank and file.*** If Government do produce such a statement it is probable that the great majority of the Armed Forces will remain reliable and prepared to do their duty in aid of the civil power.

Possible Military Commitments

9. (a) The essential military commitments are:

(i) Security of INDIA against external attack.

(ii) Maintenance of order in the tribal areas of the N.W.F. Province and Baluchistan.

(iii) Maintenance of INDIA as a base for S.E.A.C.

(iv) Maintenance of vital military communications and installations.

(v) Protection of the lives of Europeans and Indians likely to become the victims of mob violence.

(b) As regards (i) above, the only likely external threat in the immediate future is from Afghanistan, and this might well eventuate as a result of widespread disorder in India and particularly in the North West-Frontier Province. Afghan aggression would entail the reinforcement of the Frontier Defence troops thus seriously weakening the forces available to deal with internal disorder.

(c) As regards (ii) above, Government is pursuing a policy designed to ensure the peacefulness of the N.W. Frontier, but if, as is possible, there was a major Frontier rising, at least one extra division would have to be allotted to the Frontier Defence Troops as well as more aircraft.

(d) As regards (iii) above, the *possibility of concentrating the bulk of the maintenance reserves for S.E.A.C. close behind the East coast ports is being examined. If this is done, it will reduce but not eliminate the rail movement necessary to discharge our responsibility for maintenance of S.E.A.C.* Full discharge of this responsibility will still be dependent upon the security of rail communications throughout the length and breadth of India.

(e) As regards (iv) above, *plans are being coordinated at all levels for the defence of Naval Army/Air Force vital points and the maintenance of vital communications. These plans aim at ensuring that essential services of all kinds are concentrated in firm defended bases; that adequate arrangements, based on the use of wireless and air transport, are made to meet the possible dislocation of civil communications services;* that reserves are so sited in relation to likely centres of disorder and protected airfields that they can move rapidly as and when required.

As regards (v) above, it *may be necessary to arrange for the rapid concentration of European and Indian civilians requiring protection in defended areas, which will probably be based on the main protected airfields.* It is not however to be expected that all such persons can be concentrated and afforded adequate protection.

Forces Available to Meet Possible Military Commitments

10. (a) The naval forces in the East Indies Station, if placed at my disposal, would constitute a mobile reserve for the reinforcement of defended ports and a valuable alternative means of transporting troops to threatened areas.

(b) The available offensive air forces, including those at present under command of B.A.F.S.E.A., should suffice to meet any threat from Afghanistan, as well as to deal with tribal outbreaks on the North-West Frontier, and to provide support for troops employed in restoring internal order. It is however, very desirable in view of the gradual reduction of air forces in India, that *I should have a call at short notice on at least two R.A.F. fighter squadrons from A.C.S.E.A. or the Middle East.*

(c) The maximum air transportation resources now available in B.A.F.S.E.A. for use in emergency are:

Liberators Dakotas

Under Command Allotted to

B.A.F.S.E.A. Air Trooping Total

30 20 50
20 135 155

205
but these numbers are liable to fluctuate.

Taking into account the demands there are likely to be from all over India for transport aircraft for the movement of reserves, evacuation and concentration of threatened civilians, transportation of food, ammunition, stores and P.O.L., and the clearing of casualties, it is necessary that all transport aircraft that may be in India when widespread trouble starts should be immediately placed at my disposal.
Assuming that the number of transport aircraft in India does not fall below the figure given above, I estimate that *I should require not less than five additional transport squadrons to deal with major widespread disturbances.*

(d) Land Forces, British

There are sufficient British units in India to provide an adequate leaven of British troops in dealing with any internal trouble provided the Indian forces remain reliable. I consider, however, that it is necessary to retain in India two armoured regiments and certain troops of 2 Division, including artillery, which were destined for South East Asia Command.

(e) Land Forces, Indian
Taking into account the return of 10 Ind. Div. to India, there should be by next Spring sufficient troops in India to deal with

widespread internal trouble provided the reliability of the Indian Army is not affected. The return of 10 Ind. Div. will NOT however release any troops for use outside India.

CONCLUSIONS

11. *We must be prepared to deal with well organised revolution next Spring, and the possibility of a serious, but less well organised rising at any time during the coming winter.*

We must also be ready to deal with widespread and bitter intercommunal strife which might put a severe strain on the reliability of the Indian Armed Forces should they be called on to act against their own co-religionists.

12. *The reliability and spirit of the Indian Forces including the police will best be secured by a firm and explicit declaration by His Majesty's Government* to the effect that, while they maintain their intention to grant self-government to India by constitutional methods:

(i) any armed insurrection will be put down, by force if necessary and the leaders punished.

(ii) Government servants will be supported to the full.
(iii) The police and troops acting in the execution of their duty will be protected at the time and thereafter.It is realised that (iii) is open to the criticism that, *in view of the declared intention of His Majesty's Government*

to grant self-government to India, the promise of protection cannot be guaranteed. But if the present situation develops into a general armed rebellion which has to be suppressed by force, the chances of Congress extremists gaining political power in India will inevitably be postponed for a number of years.

13. *In the absence of a firm declaration the loyalty of the Indian Forces is likely progressively to deteriorate as time passes* and Congress and other bodies intensify their anti-British campaign.

14. Provided the Indian Forces, including the police, remain loyal, India has sufficient British and Indian Forces available to deal with widespread internal disturbance unless this coincides with Afghan aggression or a major rising of the tribes of the North-West Frontier.

15. Transport aircraft now available will not suffice in an extreme emergency.

16. *If the Indian Forces as a whole cease to be reliable, the British Armed Forces now available are not likely to be able to control the internal situation or to protect essential communications, nor would any piecemeal reinforcement of these forces be of much avail.*

To regain control of the situation and to restore essential communications within the country, nothing short of an organised campaign for the reconquest of India is likely to suffice.

It is *not possible now to compute the air and land forces required for such a campaign, but they would inevitably be very large as, if the Indian Armed Forces are not prepared to support*

Government, they will almost inevitably actively oppose it. Further, such active opposition is not likely to be confined to India alone. *Disaffection will inevitably spread to Indian troops now being employed by His Majesty's Government in overseas theatres such as Burma, Malaya, Java and the Middle East* with serious repercussions on the attitude of the peoples of those countries. Afghanistan also may well throw in her lot with the Frontier tribes and the Mussalmans of North Western India.

17. *The situation in India is, therefore, extremely delicate.*

If there is a widespread revolt against the Government everything will depend upon the reliability of the Indian Armed Forces. This depends upon political more than upon military factors and it is essential that our political action both in India and in the neighbouring countries where Indian troops are employed, should in no way give opportunities for political agitation to subvert the loyalty to Government of the Indian Armed Forces. Our action in Java and French Indo-China is already being represented as European repression of national risings of Eastern peoples. If this is made a major political issue as is likely, *it may have a serious effect upon the loyalty of the Indian Armed Forces.* It is certainly very undesirable that any further Indian troops should be sent to these or other similar countries. *The reliability of the Indian Armed Forces is also likely to deteriorate if Government shows any lack of confidence in them.*

While, therefore, the despatch of further British troops to India may at first sight appear attractive, I consider that reinforcement in small numbers is likely to be ineffective in the event of widespread revolt whilst the despatch now to India of large British formations may do more harm than good in that it would show lack of confidence in the Indian Armed Forces and might well precipitate a crisis which we must do everything to avoid. For the moment the most important thing is to maintain at adequate strength the cadre of experienced British officers in Indian units. The number of such officers is already being steadily reduced by repatriation and release.

Should the situation so deteriorate that we cannot rely upon the Indian Armed Forces, I may have to ask His Majesty's Government to send to India as many British formations as can be made available. In these circumstances very early despatch would be essential, as, to be effective, these reinforcements would have to arrive before the forces of violence gain control.

I request, therefore, that plans may be prepared for the despatch to India of such British Formations as could be made available in the event of a serious emergency, and that I may be informed of the possible strength of these reinforcements and of the approximate period which would elapse between the request for their despatch and their arrival in Indian ports.

It is essential that *any preparations or actual moves in this connection should be made under the guise of a plan to replace Indian Formations in the South East Asian Command by British Formations*, using India as a staging base in order to complete their organisation and equipment. Too much importance cannot be paid to this aspect of the situation as it is absolutely essential to do or say nothing which might aggravate the present extremely delicate situation, and I trust that this will be firmly impressed on all authorities concerned, both military and civilian.

II. CHIEFS OF STAFF TO GENERAL AUCHINLECK (VIA CABINET OFFICES AND SPECIAL CHANNELS)

11 DECEMBER 1945, 5.12 pm TOP SECRET
[Unnumbered)

Following from Chiefs of Staff

Reference your appreciation on internal situation in India.

1. We are confronted with the practical problem of making plans for the possible movement of British forces to India in certain eventualities. To enable us to prepare these plans it is necessary for us to have further particulars.

2. We note that *only the two extremes of complete loyalty and general disaffection in Indian Armed Forces are considered; also that you have sufficient forces in first case.* We also imagine that you must envisage a *situation, somewhere between these two extremes,* occurring and that you will be making plans to deal with it.
Before we can present the whole case, together with our [re]commendations, to His Majesty's Government, we first require to know

(a) The broad principles of your plan for dealing with internal situation caused by varying degrees of disaffection.

(b) How would British troops be employed?

This might affect the type of any formation sent.

(c) What reinforcements of land and air forces and what assistance from R.N. would be required for each stage?

(d) What phasing of movement would your plan require?

(e) How much notice do you expect to be able to give?

Reference Viceroy's telegram 2065-S- to Secretary of State for India, what are your views on reinforcements by British troops?

(g) Reference your paragraph 12. To what extent do you consider statement made on 4th December in House of Commons will allay tendency to disaffection?

3. We should also like to have further information on following points:
(a) Reference your paragraph 9 (b) and (c).

Have you any further information regarding likelihood of Afghan incursion or Frontier risings? In case of former, do you consider forces you now have available on Frontier sufficient to deal with it?

(b) Reference your paragraph 6.
We would be glad to know what steps are being taken to combat these factors. Now proclamation has been made are there any other steps which we can take here to assist in counteracting disaffection?

(c) We should like more details of your cover plan for an early introduction of British troops.

(d) To what extent do you consider you can rely on R.I.N. and Royal Indian Air Force?

(e) Reference your paragraph 10 (a). Usual degree of co-operation between Commanders-in-Chief in preparation of a plan to meet emergency should be adequate. Reference your paragraph 10 (c). We cannot reconcile your statement of air transport forces available in emergency with Air Ministry information. Request you enumerate units on availability of which you are counting.
Our worldwide resources of transport aircraft will have been drastically reduced by Spring 1946 owing to end of lend/lease.
Essential therefore that we should have details of your plans for use of transport aircraft including total requirements and proportion of twin engined aircraft necessary which will be in short supply.

4. A very early reply is requested.

5. If it would be any help, we could send you an expert in Deception to assist in its preparation. He would, of course, be on temporary loan.

III. GENERAL AUCHINLECK TO CHIEFS OF STAFF (VIA DIRECTOR OF INTELLIGENCE, INDIA AND CABINET OFFICES)

22 DECEMBER 1945, 2.45 pm

Received: 23 December, 12.22 pm TOP SECRET IMMEDIATE For Chiefs of Staff from Auchinleck.

In my appreciation I stressed great importance of maintaining reliability of Indian Armed Forces as if these remain steadfast, forces at my disposal are I consider just adequate now to deal with widespread internal disturbances. Strength of these forces will steadily increase as Indian formations return from Mideast and SEAC provided we are not forced to demobilise an equivalent number of static units.

If however Indian Armed Forces generally become unreliable British troops at my disposal are totally inadequate to restore situation or even to protect communications which would be essential for their reinforcement.

You now ask me whether there is not an intermediate stage between these two extremes and you put certain detailed questions based on the assumption that it is possible to forecast such an intermediate stage.

3. I find these questions very difficult to answer.

My present plans are based on the assumption that the bulk of the Indian Armed Forces remain reliable but that there is widespread civil disturbance throughout the country in both industrial and rural districts. This is the firm basis upon which I can make definite plans as I consider that any intermediate stage is so indeterminate as to make it impossible to assess its scope both numerically and geographically.

4. At present there are no signs that any particular class or classes (e.g., Sikhs, Pathans or Madrassis) are more likely to become disaffected than others. Nor can it be said that troops located in one part of India have shown themselves to be more susceptible to subversive propaganda than troops located in other parts. *Indian officers*

who are mostly Nationalist are spread throughout the Indian Armed Forces except in Gurkha units. Similarly the large numbers of better educated and politically conscious men referred to in my appreciation are spread throughout the technical and administrative branches of all three services and comprise men of all castes and creeds.

5. The factors affecting reliability as stated in para. 6 of my appreciation are mainly political and not repeat not military. *Congress praise of men of so-called Indian National Army as true patriots and extravagant anti-Government abuse are reaching men through civilian contacts if not also directly. Almost all units wherever stationed in India report that men are becoming aware of this propaganda.* The uneducated and ignorant are bewildered or at best indifferent. The more intelligent are beginning to wonder where their interests lie. So far there are no repeat no real indications that troops intend to abandon their allegiance to Government or would disobey orders given by their officers. If however morale were to deteriorate gravely owing to continued propaganda and *some units mutinied news would spread rapidly and mutiny might become general even if in some cases half-hearted.*

6. *Even if in these circumstances some units remain prepared to fight for Government against their own people it is impossible to foretell which these units might be and therefore where they would be located. It is likely that Gurkha units may be less affected than others as all their officers are British but Gurkhas are Hindus and not necessarily immune to Congress propaganda.* I consider therefore that it is necessary to plan on the two extremes and that the data are too imponderable to enable me to plan usefully for any intermediate stage.

7. Since forwarding my appreciation Congress Working Committee has met in Calcutta and there are signs of a definite change in the attitude of the propaganda of political leaders have become more sober and less inflammatory. This may be due to premature disturbances in Calcutta and to statements in House of Commons on 4 December and by Viceroy on 10 December. These statements should go some way towards combating disaffection as well as acting as welcome brake upon extremist political leaders but it is too early yet to assess their actual effect on Indian troops. I am taking necessary steps to be sure that their statements are brought to notice of all troops.

8. *Congress now show signs of realising that any serious deterioration in the discipline and obedience to authority of the Indian Armed Forces would not be in their own interest should they assume power and that it would be better to try first to gain this power by constitutional means rather than by insurrection. At the moment therefore it seems likely that there will be no repeat no widespread disturbances organised by existing political leaders before April 1946*, that they are improbable before. Situation however is liable to sudden changes and is naturally being kept under constant review.

9. Disturbances might be precipitated by Govt. action e.g. arrest of leaders, or they might be result of secret orders and be carefully timed. In latter case we might get no or only very short warning.

10. Replies to your remaining questions, in so far as I can reply to them, follow in my immediately succeeding signal.

TOP SECRET

IV. GENERAL AUCHINLECK TO CHIEFS OF STAFF (VIA DIRECTOR OF INTELLIGENCE, INDIA AND CABINET OFFICES)

22 DECEMBER 1945, 2.47 pm Received: 23 December; 12.21 pm

1. Gradual introduction now of British infantry and possibly artillery units would certainly be a logical sequel to Government's declared intention to support its loyal servants, and apparent changed attitude of Congress may create favourable opportunity. But we are not dealing with logic so much as with ill will of political leaders who are prepared to discard truth for political ends and who have means of spreading propaganda verbally by agents. This is very difficult to counter amongst largely illiterate people by presentation of truth in Press even if Press were willing to help by giving necessary publicity. *If, for example, Congress took line that arrival of British troops was due to distrust of Indian units and British troops were intended to disarm Indian troops and coerce Indian people we should precipitate trouble rather than prevent it.*

2. If British troops are sent before disturbances begin they must be preceded by thorough deception plan. I should welcome visit by deception expert but must emphasise that plan must be political rather than military and must be acceptable to Indian Armed Forces and Indian people. Possible line might be that British troops were en route to NEI to relieve Indian troops.

V. GENERAL AUCHINLECK TO FIELD MARSHAL VISCOUNT ALANBROOKE

14 February 1946
MOST IMMEDIATE
TOP SECRET

Regret delay in replying but Viceroy and I have both been on tour.

My view of situation is as follows:
FIRST, It is not possible to make an accurate and satisfactory appreciation on ordinary military lines because no one can forecast with any certainty the extent or degree of the hostile action with which we may have to deal.

Such action *may vary from complete rebellion aided by the whole or great majority of the Indian Armed Forces and supported by the tribes of the North-West Frontier to isolated civil disturbances in different parts of the country in suppression of which it may be possible to use Indian Armed Forces in support of the Indian Police.*_

Between these two extremes there are an infinite number of intermediate crises which might arise which cannot be defined with military accuracy thus making it impossible to draw up plans to meet every contingency.

SECOND, In addition to the above possibilities of anti-Government action there is the equally if not *more serious possibility of a religious war on a large scale and covering the greater part of India between Hindus and Moslems.*_

This contingency is becoming more dangerous as time goes on and should it arise will be extremely difficult to meet as it is more than likely that it *will be impossible to rely on either the Police or the Indian Armed Forces to take action for the restoration of law and order if this means firing on their own co-religionists.*

This means that British troops alone would be available to restore the situation and certainly result in turning communal strife into anti-Government action by both parties.

In this event we would again be faced by the risk of the India[n] Armed Forces throwing in their lot with the insurgent elements as there is little doubt that the rank and file of these forces would have been badly shaken and disturbed by the initial communal strife.

THIRD, *It can be realised therefore that if the worst comes to the worst British troops will be the only stable element in the country and that unless the essential key points can be held with reasonable certainty the maintenance of these troops may well become impossible.*_

These ***key points are in my opinion the capital Delhi whence alone control can be exercised and the four chief ports Bombay Karachi Calcutta and Madras.***

FOURTH, I have at present following British troops available:

Infantry Battalions Armoured Regiments Artillery Regiments
17 plus about one hundred thousand British personnel in Staffs Engineer Signal and Administrative units Transit Camps Training Centres etc. There are also the RAF personnel distributed throughout India but not really organised for action.

FIFTH, In the circumstances and especially in view of the complete *uncertainty as to the political outcome of the present most confused situation in India it is impossible for me to say that the immediate despatch of three British Brigade Groups to India is essential.*

I can and do say that *as an insurance their despatch would be desirable in order to minimise any risk there may be of loss of control of the key points mention(ed)* in my Fourth [Third] above.

The need for Brigade Groups as opposed to Brigades will I think be evident from my estimate of the possibilities inherent in the situation but it is possible that I could add to the Infantry the necessary Artillery and other units from forces already in India.

It can be *argued that the arrival of these Brigades might have a steadying effect but I am not convinced myself that this would necessarily be so and I doubt if this is sufficient justification for their despatch.*

SIXTH, Please pass copy of this to General Mayne.

6

Conclusive Evidence: The Viceroy Fd Mshl Viscount Wavell's Correspondence

Another most critical decision maker of the empire was the Viceroy Fd Mshl Viscount Archibald Wavell—a great military Commander who had earned fame in the North Africa theatre. Wavell was the Viceroy of India from 1943 to 1947. It is noteworthy that before he had been moved out to take charge of the Middle East Theatre of war he had been Commander-in-Chief India. As such he knew India very well. Fd marshal Claude Auchinleck had served most of his military career in India and was Commander-in-Chief India from 1943 to 1947. These then were the most experienced India hands who were serving together in India at the time of independence. They were men who knew the Indian army very well and had practically grown with this army. They were sensitive to the major changes taking place in this army—changes that had been catalysed by the impact of Bose and his INA. The INA trials designed to overawe the Indian army had backfired badly. These two experienced Generals had to deal with this impact and they showed great maturity and tact. This is reflected in their correspondence and reports. The letter below talks of the reports on the post INA trial riots especially in Calcutta where transport infrastructure was attacked. It talks of not using Indian troops to quell revolts against the Dutch in the Java and French indo-China. He clearly mentions that he fully endorses Auchinleck's appreciation of the situation.

VICEROY FIELD MARSHAL VISCOUNT WAVELL'S REPORT TO SECRETARY OF STATE LORD PETHICK-LAWRENCE

The report is given here as it appeared in "Transfer of Power," Volume 6, page 552.

I. FIELD MARSHAL VISCOUNT WAVELL TO
LORD PETHICK-LAWRENCE
THE VICEROY'S HOUSE, NEW DELHI,

27 NOVEMBER 1945
PRIVATE AND SECRET

Thank you for your letter of the 16th November. Since you wrote we have exchanged telegrams about the political situation, and I have had to say that I do not entirely agree with the suggestions that have been made for reducing the tension. Perhaps your most important suggestion was that I should see Gandhi.
The difficulty is that even if this did good with the Congress, it would immediately do corresponding harm with the Muslims and tend to redouble their suspicions. Also Gandhi and Congress would at once try to make a bargain and would use my approach as propaganda. I feel I should try to keep on an absolutely even keel for the time being and do nothing which suggests a tendency either to give way to threats of the Congress or to encourage the intransigence of the Muslim League. As for the proposal that Nehru and Jinnah should go to London I think the chief objection to it is that there is really no chance whatever of their accepting it. The Muslim League could not possibly manage the elections without Jinnah, and Jinnah would consider that if he and Nehru both went, the Muslim League would lose everything whereas the Congress would lose one of a number of efficient

electioneering politicians. Also, Nehru is so angry with Jinnah for his behaviour at Simla that he would not be likely to be amenable in discussions with him even in London, apart from the fact that he is committed to a no compromise policy and could not afford to look as though he was going back on it during the elections. This last point of course applies to Jinnah equally. And of course Nehru is not the official head of Congress, as would be pointed out to us.

2. I like your draft announcement in Parliament, and though I have suggested a rearragement you will see that I have suggested no additions except a reference to the recent disturbances. It is, however, important from our point of view here that the primary object of the statement should be to announce His Majesty's Government's determination not to permit violence. The rest on this occasion should be subsidiary. The impression that statements of this sort make in India depends so much more on their tone than on the actual words that an apparently minor rearrangement may be important.

3. *You have no doubt seen Auchinleck's appreciation for the Chiefs of Staff. I think it is a good appreciation and have told you in a telegram that I agree with almost all of it*, though I have suggested a reservation on one point.

4. Casey flew up to see me on Sunday afternoon and went back the next day. I had a long talk to him about the *Calcutta riots*. They seem to have been in two phases.

The first was the procession of students which was stopped by the police; Casey describes it as a collection of quite hysterical young men, with whom it was impossible to reason, but who were not violent; they eventually dispersed, probably from sheer exhaustion, after some 15 hours shouting and demonstrating.

The feature of *the next phase was attacks on all forms of transport, large numbers of lorries and private cars being stopped and burnt, road blocks formed across many of the streets, and some of the railway lines stopped by crowds sitting on them.*

There was no obvious connection between the two phases, but there was certainly a good deal of organisation behind the second phase; it looks as if some of the extreme elements had taken advantage of the first phase to attack the transport system possibly as a dress rehearsal for something bigger later on; possibly in the hope that something big might develop of itself. This phase also ended as suddenly and unaccountably as it had begun.

On top of all this was the strike of the Calcutta Corporation employees, which was purely an industrial dispute and had no connection with the riots, but naturally added to the difficulties and anxieties of the Government.

Casey was impressed by the very strong anti-British feeling behind the whole demonstration, and considers the whole situation still very explosive and dangerous.

The root cause of it all, he thinks and I agree, lies in the inflammatory speeches of the political leaders during the last month or two, working on the unstable minds of the youthful Bengali. So long as this violent speaking goes on, we shall have to expect outbreaks of this kind.

Though one American was killed (burned alive in an ambulance) and a number injured, Casey does not think the Americans were in any way specially attacked; he says they behaved with admirable restraint, and carried out his requests to keep off the streets during the trouble as far as possible. Casey was not impressed by the methods or staff work of the police. He intends to hold an official enquiry on the firing, and to overhaul the police arrangements. He is sending one of his officers down to Bombay to study their procedure for dealing with crowds and disturbances. I think Casey himself handled the affair admirably, and that without him it might have developed more seriously.

5. *The need for a firm attitude about violence has been brought home to me by a recent intelligence report I have received.*

The following are some extracts from a single day's report:

In the course of *one meeting at Nagpur, R. S. Ruikar threatened the British Government that if mercy was not shown to the I.N.A. personnel, Indians would not spare their last drop of blood in saving their lives and asked the people to hold themselves in readiness for a movement "more powerful and mightier than that of 1942."*

"In Delhi, large handwritten posters in red ink recently appeared *threatening death for 'twenty English dogs' for every I.N.A. man executed." In the Central Provinces, the President of the Mahakoshal Provincial Congress Committee is reported to have stated privately that the movement which Congress now visualised, unless Gandhi gave a clear-cut directive to the contrary, would not only be of a violent character but would be reinforced by the co-operation of released I.N.A. personnel and other revolutionary elements trained in guerilla warfare; he declared another movement inevitable.*

6. The I.N.A. trials are in progress again, and it is becoming more and more clear that the distorted publicity which has attended them is doing a very great deal of harm to Government and constitutes a threat to the morale of the Indian Army. All parties have taken the same line though Congress are more vociferous than the others. It cannot fail to be disturbing to the Indian Army to find that the vocal part of the country at any rate has an entirely different set of values from that which the Indian Army has been taught to observe.

There are undoubtedly many ex-prisoners of war who are extremely angry and resentful about this hero worship of traitors, but the great bulk of vocal opinion is the other way. One of the troubles in India is that the opinion that is heard is only that of a very small urban population which, though it is very far from being representative of the whole country, monopolises the press and the platform.

One trouble is that *the evidence against the accused in the present trial, at any rate on the first few days, has not been such as to horrify the normal Indian in any way. The Congress cry has been that these men only loved their country too well.* It would have been much better if we had brought on first the trials in which the accused were alleged to be guilty of the grossest brutality to other Indians.

But even when evidence of brutality comes out, as it has done lately, the Nationalist papers hide it unobtrusively on a back page and headline some sentence or phrase favourable to their thesis. The effect of the trials has been discussed in the last few days by police representatives from the Provinces and then by the Commander-in-Chief and G.H.Q.

As the result I have accepted a revised policy of which you will have heard by telegram. We have decided in effect to proceed only, apart from the present trial, with cases in which there are allegations of brutality, and a communique has been put out which makes our intentions clear. The present trial will still undoubtedly present opportunities, before it is finished, of rubbing in the anti-British propaganda and attacking the morale of the Indian army. But the first of the brutality trials is to start on the 3rd December, and the way will be less clear for the propagandists when the evidence in that case is also before the public.

The I.N.A. trials have been embarrassing, but I think the use of Indian troops in Java and French Indo-China is more damaging in the long run because the case against it is, from the Indian point of view, almost a cast-iron one, and there is little need to twist the arguments in order to make it look wrong.

Mountbatten has been here for the last day or two, and although the whole situation is, I realise, extremely embarrassing and difficult for His Majesty's Government, *I do support his request for a clear and unequivocal statement of policy.* Bevin did his best in his speech of the

23rd November but that speech made it clear, I think, that His Majesty's Government had still not decided whether our task in Java is really "rescue only" or is also the holding of a secure base through which the Dutch can pass and from which they may be able to re-establish their control. From what Mountbatten told me I should think it is next to impossible for the Dutch to re-establish control, and the sooner we make a clear-cut decision the better.

If we manage to rescue the internees the Dutch can hardly say that we have let them down entirely, and on a sober appreciation of the job to be done they must admit that it is no business of ours to take a large part in it. In case, as Mountbatten said in one of his telegrams, there *is a clear time-limit to the use of Indian troops in Java, and I must continue to press for their withdrawal with the minimum delay.*

VICEROY FIELD MARSHAL VISCOUNT WAVELL'S REPORTS TO H. M. THE KING AND PRIME MINISTER MR. ATTLEE

The reports are given here as they appeared in "Transfer of Power," Volume 6, pages 713, 1054.

I. FIELD MARSHAL VISCOUNT WAVELL TO H.M. THE KING GEORGE VI (EXTRACT)
WAVELL PAPERS, PRIVATE CORRESPONDENCE: H.M.THE KING, PP. 100-2
THE VICEROY'S HOUSE, NEW DELHI

31 DECEMBER 1945

Your Majesty,
It is just two months since I last wrote. They have been quite busy and eventful months. I have

done a good deal of touring and there have been some developments in the political situation.

2. *The troubles* which I feared might be brought about by the intemperate speeches of Nehru and other Congress leaders, with their indiscriminate championship of the I.N.A. and glorification of the "martyrs" of August 1942, *duly occurred in Calcutta in the last week of November, when serious rioting broke out which might easily have developed much more seriously still. It began with a students' procession in favour of the I.N.A. which defied police orders; and ended four days later, suddenly and rather mysteriously, when the mob was almost out of hand, transport in Calcutta was practically paralysed,* and the troops were standing by to take over from the Police. The tale of the casualties and damage shows how dangerous the situation had become: *33 killed* (one an American lorry-driver burned to death, the remainder civilians); *nearly 200 Police, Fire Brigade and soldiers (70 British, 37 American), and about 200 civilians injured; 150 military or police vehicles and a large number of civilian cars destroyed or damaged.* Casey handled the situation admirably, but the Police staff work and tactics showed obvious weaknesses.

3. *These riots proved a turning-point in the immediate political situation,* and caused at least a temporary detente. The leaders realised that the violence of their speeches were [was] likely to cause outbreaks of violence a result which had been obvious to everyone else for some time; and that the authorities were quite prepared and determined to put down such outbreaks with a firm hand—a purpose which was reinforced by the statements in Parliament and by a speech I made at Calcutta. Gandhi, who had been apparently

hibernating for some time, now took a hand, and at one reasserted his influence over Congress. He is believed to have issued orders that violence and incitements to violence are to be avoided, until after the elections at any rate. *Although the speeches of Nehru and Co. and the statements in the Nationalist Press would still be termed rank sedition and provocation of rebellion in most countries, they have lately been moderate compared with those of a month or two ago.*

4. Gandhi has had a series of conversations with Casey. They began with a natural wish on Casey's part to meet Gandhi when he came to Bengal, and have continued at the request of the old man, who seems to enjoy talking at large to Casey. Casey gave me a detailed account of his last conversation; it ranged from such domestic subjects as the drunken habits of one of his sons, the soothing effect to being massaged with mustard oil and lemon, and the economic advantages of home spinning, to the wrongs done to India by Warren Hastings and Clive and the evils that would follow from Pakistan. He said of Pakistan that His Majesty's Government must make up its mind between those who had always opposed us (Congress) but who now wanted the right thing, a united India, and those who had helped us, the Muslims, but wanted a wrong thing, a divided India. Gandhi had said very much the same to me at our last interview at Simla, six months ago.

I had a 40 minutes talk with Gandhi myself three weeks ago, in which he was quite friendly but rather vague and woolly, giving me a long dissertation on the eventual conquest of the world by his doctrine of non-violence. Immediately afterwards he had a talk with Arthur Smith, to whom he sang a hymn of hate against the

British and all their works, ranging from the Mutiny to the Simla Conference last summer. He is an odd mixture of benevolence (outward) and malevolence (inward).
I should put the composition of his character as 70% extremely astute politicism, with a fixed dislike of the British and determination to rid India of them; 15% saint and 15% charlatan. I am always pretty clear about the first of these percentages, but my estimate of the second and third proportions changes frequently.

5. There has been no real change of heart in Congress, but I think they have changed their tactics to the extent of trying to avoid any outbreak until after the elections; so that we may perhaps have a comparatively peaceful month or two ahead; though there is so much inflammable material about, and such fiery sound still issues from Congress speeches, that there might easily be a premature explosion.
Interest in the I.N.A. trials, which might well cause such an explosion, has for the time being died down. Congress, having succeeded in creating a picture of the I.N.A. men as high-minded partiots, is now inclined to withdraw the limelight lest the picture be spoilt by the evidence of some of their patriotic excesses such as the murder and torture of those who stood loyal. As soon as the first verdicts and sentences are given in the next few days, the whole weight of the Nationalist Press will again be directed towards securing their release or at least the commutation of their sentences.

6. I am not very much looking forward to 1946. It is difficult to see how any agreement is to be secured between Congress and Muslim League on the composition of a new Executive Council

or of a Constitution making-Convention; and, failing agreement, how a conflict of some sort is to be avoided. I believe someone once described golf as "getting a small ball into a hole with instruments singularly ill-adapted for the purpose." The political leaders in India, Gandhi, Jinnah, Nehru and the others, are certainly singularly ill-adapted for delicate constitutional negotiation and will almost inevitably land one in the rough or some very deep bunkers. We must somehow secure agreement and avoid an upheaval, which would be a great deal more serious than in 1942; but I confess that I don't quite know how it is going to be done. I feel rather like a Wild Western poker player going into a game with a carefully loaded gun on the most handy part of his person, while devoutly hoping he will not have to use it.

II. FIELD MARSHAL VISCOUNT WAVELL TO MR. ATTLEE (VIA INDIA OFFICE)

NEW DELHI, 24 February 1946 4.50 pm
Received: 24 February, 1.25 pm MOST IMMEDIATE
Following personal for Prime Minister from Viceroy.

1. Full information of events has been telegraphed home from here and Bombay and there seems no use in my recapitulating them. *Naval mutiny is now under control and, I hope, ended. But rioting by mobs in Bombay is serious and situation is still unstable.* It is early yet to attempt appreciation but following represents my judgement up to date.

2. Primary cause of whole trouble is of (sic) speeches by Congress leaders since September last.

As I have warned them publicly and privately on many occasions, *the preaching of violence to an excitable_people can only result eventually in disastrous violence, and idea that it can be controlled by words as easily as it is excited by words is an illusion. I am pretty sure that the top leaders of Congress had nothing to do with inciting this mutiny and did not wish it. Gandhi has put out good statement condemning violence.* But I think some of smaller Congress fry had a good deal to do with it and probably also Communist agitators.

3. *Commander-in-Chief thinks, and I agree, that events do not indicate any inherent rottenness in R.I.N. R.I.N. has not same background as army, proportion of experienced officers and petty officers is very small owing to rapid expansion during war, and number of young and excitable men have been worked on by agitators from inside and outside. There may have been service grievances but I do not think they were serious.* Spirit is still probably good if men are well handled. I am afraid that *example of the Royal Air Force, who got away with what was really a mutiny, has some responsibility for present situation.*

4. I think that *personnel of the R.I.A.F. attached to R.A.F. have probably more serious grievances from service point of view than R.I.N. They have, as you know, only become responsibility of the C.-in-C. India very lately and their conditions of service are being examined urgently.*

5. Welfare of army and any legitimate grievances have been under constant review of C. and authorities, I think I can safely say, for whole period of war and since it. I do not believe

there is any really serious material (corrupt group) [?cause] for agitation, but *unless Indian soldier is paid at same rates as British, which is not possible, agitators may always allege racial discrimination.*

6. *There will be no victimisation but ringleaders of this deplorably mutiny must of course receive proper punishment. C.-in-C. proposed to establish fact-finding court of enquiry to determine actual course of events and to recommend a high-level committee of enquiry into the causes of outbreak.* I agree that this is correct course.

7. So much for the military side. *The civil disturbances [?followed] much the usual pattern. There are in Bombay and Calcutta and all large Indian towns (and in the countryside too in a lesser degree) numerous dangerous elements who take immediate advantage of any disturbed conditions to begin rioting and looting. At the end of January 1946 brief strikes took place in 12 R.A.F. stations in the East as a protest at the slow rate of demobilisation. Earlier in the month similar repatriation protests had been made by members of U.S. forces stationed in India and elsewhere.* Indian political leaders use these mobs for their own ends, and are then surprised and alarmed that they break out on their own. *They are probably being incited at present by left-wing Congress and Communists against the intention of more responsible leaders.* The issue is uncertain, but I am sure we can control it.

8. *By set attitude to I.N.A. trials, Congress and Moslem League have aroused passions which they are now quite unable to regulate. It is impossible to get any reasonable view taken by average educated Indian on this subject.* But I am sure we cannot

at present (?change) our policy, which is already generous. Sentence of 7 years R.I. on I.N.A. (?officer) who had man suspended from rope and beaten senseless will be promulgated on Monday and may cause further cases of which the results will have to be announced from time to time.

9. The above is (?mentioned) as a personal expression of opinion based at present on information which is necessarily incomplete. It is not meant as a brief for a statement in Parliament. I will cable further this evening or tomorrow morning if anything fresh occurs.

Comments

The above letter is addressed to the Prime Minister Lord Attlee and reports to him about the Naval mutiny. There is less alarm in these reports compared to the aftermath of the INA trials. This does occur as a process of habituation to a set of reports or circumstances. However the naval mutiny was a self-fulfilling prophecy and clearly indicated to the rulers in London that the local commanders in India had a good grasp of the situation and their appreciation and estimates were largely correct. Frankly Fd Mshal Auchinleck's Appreciation in November 1945 had clearly anticipated problems arising as early as February 1946 and that is precisely when the RIN Mutiny had erupted. London was now quite convinced that the situation in India was headed for disaster and it would be prudent to head off serious trouble by an early announcement of the grant of independence. The Congress leaders were equally alarmed and we find them collaborating with the British to douse out the flames of the Indian Naval mutiny. They had bargained so long for a transfer of power to themselves and were worried that it would slip out of their control entirely now at this belated stage. They actively collaborated with the British in dousing the flames of the Naval mutiny. Nehru and Patel spoke to the leaders of the mutiny to persuade them to surrender peacefully. This is what seems to have calmed frayed

British nerves for a bit. The writing was now clearly on the wall. The centre of gravity of British colonial rule in India was the loyalty of the native sepoy to the Raj. This was now completely gone. Bose and the INA had effectively torpedoed this loyalty of the native sepoy to a moribund Raj. The British success at nativisation was now a thing of the past.

It was time for the Raj to leave.

7

Reports of the Provincial Governors

Introduction

The third set of critical decision makers in India were the British Governors of the various provinces. In this chapter we examine a set of Reports from the Governors to the Viceroy about the situation in their own respective provinces just before and after the INA trials in November- December 1945. These reports are noteworthy for their tone of genuine alarm and apprehension. No doubt these ground reports deeply influenced the Viceroy's perception of the situation and reinforced his own sense of great unease—which had finally impelled him to virtually give an ultimatum to London to make a substantive announcement about Independence. In the absence of such a commitment, he was very clear that time was running out for the British empire in India. It could at best hold on for another 18 months (till June 1948). After that the Raj could well lose the power to influence events on the ground in India. It was better to depart with grace than get involved in a running battle. Thus:

Sir Twynam—Governor, Central Provinces—warned in end November 1945: " I do feel *uneasiness as to the attitude Indian troops might adopt if called upon to fire on mobs.* He compares the situation to the days of the mutiny and recollects how units which were thought to be perfectly loyal suddenly decided to throw their lot with the mutineers. He lists out the total number of British officials that he had to cover an area of 100,000 sq miles in the face of 18 million hostile Indians and finds them woefully in adequate.

Sir G. Cunnigham, Governor, NWFP: recommended around the same time that, "The Commander-in-Chief should immediately call off the trials as the thing is becoming more and more Indians versus the British. He commiserates: *"I feel terribly for your Excellency and for Claude A (Commander-in-Chief) in this. It is the most difficult problem to tackle that I have ever known in India. The best thing to do ... is to cut our losses."*

Sir A. Hope, Governor Madras: Stated in December 1945: *"We have put ourselves in an impossible situation_...* a tremendous attempt has been made to make *national heroes of the INA* and the attempt has had considerable success among a large and emotionally unstable section of the public. If the accused are executed or given long terms of imprisonment, *there is the danger of a popular outburst. The cardinal error was made by bringing these men to India* and not dealing with the leaders in summary courts martial on the spot. He talks of *widespread feelings of fear amongst Europeans in Ooty who are fearing serious disturbances, mutiny, etc.*

Mr. Casey, Governor, Bengal: He described in January 1946 the impact of the serious disturbances in Calcutta from November 21-23, 1945. He stated:_*"31 were killed and 179 wounded.* The forces actually employed were always hopelessly outnumbered and often in a very tight corner in the face of an *unusually determined and fanatical mob.* The most disturbing feature of these riots he pointed out was that: *The crowds when fired on generally stood their ground or at most receded just a little, to return again to the attack.*

Sir B. Glancy, Governor, Punjab: Wrote in January 1946: The conclusion of the INA trial and the arrival of these three "heroes" in Lahore gave rise to a continual orgy of extravagant welcomes, speeches and entertainments. *One disturbing feature is the attendance of Indian army personnel in uniform at meetings held in honour of the accused.*

Below I am adducing the full text of these letters from the Governors of the provinces to the Viceroy. They provide excellent documentary evidence of the overwhelming psychological impact of the INA trials and their violent aftermath on the minds of the British administration in India. Truly this is convincing and clinching evidence to settle this historical dispute on the nature and scale of psychological impact that decisively shaped British decision making before the grant of independence.

SOME GOVERNOR'S REPORT ON I.N.A. TRIALS

The reports are given here as they appeared in "Transfer of Power," Volume 6, pages 542, 546, 631, 724, 807.

I. SIR H. TWYNAM (CENTRAL PROVINCES AND BERAR) TO FIELD MARSHAL VISCOUNT WAVELL (EXTRACT)

GOVERNOR'S CAMP, CENTRAL
PROVINCES AND BERAR

SECRET

26 NOVEMBER 1945

Ruikar has been very prominent at meetings and has declared if any I.N.A. men are executed 20 patriots will arise and that the atrocities committed by the British surpassed the horrors of the Belsen Concentration Camp. I am having his speech examined with a view to a possible prosecution under the ordinary law. At Jubbulpore when a speaker said that the I.N.A. was the army of Congress and asked who would join, all raised their hands.

From the same source it is reported that Congress is jubilant at the by folly Government in trying the I.N.A. men at Delhi. Congressmen consider that this has given them a chance to win the support of the Indian Army. I am bound to say that *I do feel some uneasiness as to the attitude which Indian troops may adopt if called upon to fire on mobs. The disposition towards a sudden change of attitude in a tense political atmosphere is present now, I think, as it was in the days of the mutiny.* I have recently been reading some of the original reports printed in select State documents and extremely interesting they are. *It is extraordinary how Units which were thought to be perfectly loyal suddenly decided to throw in their lot with the mutineers.*

I do not for one moment suggest that there is any widespread disposition on these lines but a slight uneasiness remains in my mind when I envisage the possibility of the Province being completely denuded of British troops. My Special Branch officer reports that his impression is that sympathy for the I.N.A. varies inversely according to the degree of close association with the war; the closer the association the less the sympathy. He also reports that so far our Police force are apparently not interested.

2. A former Congress Minister in this Province, one D. K. Mehta, claims that Congress has many adherents among Government officials probably exists. The effect, of course, of the recent campaign is most marked on our European Government servants and many of them are undoubtedly unsettled. At present, in this Province, I have 3 European Commissioners, 5 Deputy Commissioners, no Sessions Judges, no Assistant Commissioners

and 7 District Superintendents of Police. Altogether I have available 17 European I.C.S. officers, including 3 Judicial officers, and 19 European members of the Indian Police. These figures exclude people serving in the Government of India but include people on leave.

This handful of Europeans has to deal with a population of 18 or more millions over an area of 100,000 square miles. It will be readily appreciated how difficult it will be for the administration if the present "hymn of hate" leads to the retirement of any substantial proportion of this handful of officers. Possibly the efforts of the Provincial Governors and others to secure a more moderate atmosphere may be reinforced when the Secretary of State makes his expected statement in Parliament.

II. SIR G. CUNNINGHAM (NORTH-WEST FRONTIER PROVINCE) TO FIELD MARSHAL VISCOUNT WAVELL

WAVELL PAPERS. OFFICIAL CORRESPONDENCE: INDIA, JANUARY-DECEMBER 1945, Pages 383-84

PESHAWAR, 27 NOVEMBER 1945

SECRET

Dear Lord Wavell,

I am going somewhat outside my proper sphere in writing to Your Excellency about the I.N.A. trial, but the matter is one on which I have been trying to gauge opinion of all sorts and I have now come to a definite conclusion. It is that *the C.-in-C. should at once announce that, as Indian opinion is opposed to the trial of these persons, he wipes the whole thing out and takes no further proceedings against anyone.* No one can do it but the C.-in-C., of his own volition and on his own responsibility. Done by anyone else, even by the King, it will not have the same effect—particularly on the Army. Some Army Officers of great experience with whom I have discussed the matter—Dick O' Connor was one—have said that leniency at this stage would have a disastrous effect on the Army. I do not believe that is true.

Some Indian officers and soldiers, whose relations or close friends have suffered under the I.N.A. leaders, are no doubt thirsting for their blood.

But I am certain that they are comparatively few and that their resentment at any clemency shown now would not affect Army discipline as a whole.

Most Indian soldiers who have said to me "Hang the lot" have, in my opinion, said so because they thought it was what I wanted to hear; and this applies to comment by Indians on most occasions.

The thing is daily becoming more and more purely Indian versus British, and less and less ill-disposed Indians versus British-cum-well-disposed Indians.

I think that every day that passes now brings over more and more well-disposed Indians into the anti-British camp and, whatever the outcome of the trial may be, this anti-British bias will persist in each man's mind.
The only way of stopping the rot is by a clean cut, as I have said, and at once.

I dislike saying this intensely. It is tantamount to surrendering to threats, and no reasonable man doubts for a moment that the worst of the I.N.A. leaders ought to have been shot out of hand.

Congressmen—Dr. Khan Sahib among them—have said to me, "If only they had been shot in Rangoon or Singapore, everyone would have been pleased."

But that feeling has gone and cannot now be revived.

I feel terribly for Your Excellency and for Claude A. in this.
It is the most difficult problem to tackle that I have ever known in India. But I am certain, from what I have heard from a very wide variety of people here, British and Indian, that the best thing to do is to cut our losses.

Yours sincerely, G. CUNNINGHAM

III. SIR A. HOPE (MADRAS) TO FIELD MARSHAL VISCOUNT WAVELL (EXTRACT)

GUINDY, 10 DECEMBER 1945 SECRET

2. Closely linked with the election campaign has been the question of the I.N.A. trials. After the trouble in Madura, where the police opened fire, I thought it wise to ban all meetings and processions held primarily in sympathy with the I.N.A. prisoners; but, naturally, they were bound to find their way into general election speeches. Intelligent opinion here is bewildered or jubilant, according to the political outlook of the person concerned. The general view is that we have handed first-rate election propaganda to the parties at large and that the Congress are making the most of it—in spite of their statements to

the contrary—as a focal point of expressing nationalist feeling against the British.

Secondly, it is considered that *we have put ourselves in an impossible situation*; thanks to Nehru & Co., whose example is being followed down here, *a tremendous attempt has been made to make national heroes of the I.N.A. and the attempt has had considerable success among a large and emotionally unstable section of the public._*
If the accused are executed or given long terms of imprisonment, there is the danger of a popular outburst; if, on the other hand, they are pardoned we shall be letting down our loyal men, with the result that they may well feel that loyalty does not pay. People here do not see what the solution can be, and they consider that the cardinal error was made by bringing these men to India and not dealing with the leaders in summary courts martial on the spot.

Europeans, particularly in Ootacamund, are getting very jumpy indeed and I hear about people who had intended staying on for a year or so more wanting to get passages earlier *for fear of serious disturbances, mutiny, etc._*

This sounds unjustifiably alarmist, but it is quite a widespread feeling.

IV. MR. CASEY (BENGAL) TO FIELD MARSHAL VISCOUNT WAVELL

CALCUTTA, 2 JANUARY 1946

Disturbances in Calcutta & Howrah, 21st to 23rd November 1945

My dear Lord Wavell

I have already forwarded to you with my telegram No.413 of the 28th November the text of a factual statement about these disturbances which was subsequently issued to the Press for publication on the 30th November.

(For convenience of reference I enclose a copy).

The Commissioner of Police has now completed the prescribed inquiries into the fourteen separate incidents in which firing was resorted to by the Calcutta Police and I have also just seen his report on the disturbances as a whole. In the light of these there is little to say by way of modification of that contemporary statement which, I believe, still gives a reliable picture of the course of events both in Calcutta and in Howrah. So far as Howrah is concerned I have nothing to add, and the following observations primarily concern Calcutta.

2. It is now clear that the initial clash with the Police, in Dharamtala Street on the afternoon of the 21st November, while it was deliberately sought by the students concerned was not the result of a widespread conspiracy to plunge Calcutta into anarchy.
The student organisation which sponsored the meeting and procession had been warned on both 20th and 21st November that entry into the prohibited area would not be permitted. The procession was a deliberate act of defiance of authority by students, primarily those associated with Subhas Bose's Forward Block, worked up to a state bordering on hysteria by previous propaganda in favour of the I.N.A.

3. It is not clear that the student element in the original procession was the first in the crowd to have recourse to brickbats but it is clear that, in the trial of patience between themselves and the police, the students' patience ran out first and they precipitated the riot by trying to force the cordon and attacking the police.

When defiance had led to bloodshed it was not difficult for the students, in the prevailing exacerbation of public feeling, to bring about widespread disturbances. Once rioting had commenced, students took their full share in it.

4. The two incidents, of 21st and 22nd November, in Dharamtala were primarily student processions; though naturally a considerable accretion of hangers-on, supporters and hooligans joined in when trouble began. The students also were the principal agency by which the stoppage of all means of transport was enforced next day though in this they were speedily assisted by other elements, including a number of Sikh taxi drivers, the trams were taken off the streets by the active intervention of the communist-controlled tramway men's Union.
Interference with transport was at first mainly by persuasion, though backed, of course, by threat of force. As the day proceeded, interference became steadily more violent in character. The students must bear their share of the blame for this but the actual violence was probably perpetrated more often by Sikhs, "upcountry" mechanics and the hooligan element generally. This is particularly true of the area most affected, Bhowanipore, in South Calcutta. The mobs in North Calcutta contained a higher proportion of students and bhadralog and were definitely less dangerous, less expert and apparently less determined than

those in South Calcutta where (including the two Dharamtala incidents) thirteen of the fourteen shooting incidents occurred.

5. Both in North and South Calcutta a feature of the disturbances comparatively new to Bengal was that *the crowds when fired on largely stood their ground or at most only receded a little, to return again to the attack.* This is partly because firing was carried out mainly with revolvers and in self-defence, by small groups of sergeants detached from support or operating for the extrication of wounded persons (often military personnel hauled off lorries) or to extinguish burning vehicles. There was comparatively little firing to disperse the crowds finally. The armed forces were not called upon to open fire for this purpose. The comparatively sudden collapse of the disturbances, though apparently capable of bearing a somewhat sinister implication, seems in fact attributable not to unified planning and control of the whole movement but to the interaction of a number of factors. Chief among these was the fact that the disorders, coming at the moment they did, suited the book of none of the main political parties. *Some Congress leaders from the first tried to restrain the violence of the student element, without initial success.* Throughout the forenoon and early afternoon of the 23rd, Congress and some Communist propaganda cars toured the affected areas dissuading the students from further participation. At the same time resolute action by the police in clearing roadblocks on the morning of the 23rd, the warning in the Press the same morning that adequate steps had been taken to protect military vehicles and property and a broadcast I gave that night (in which I made it plain that we should not shrink from utilising the armed forces in support of the civil power)

all had their part in bringing about the sudden collapse of the trouble and the speedy return to normal conditions.

6. So far as casualties and damage are concerned the figures given in the Statement already published may be taken as substantially correct, as will appear from the revised statement enclosed. On the side of the rioters, hospital records show that *31 were killed* (all by gunshot): of those 27 are definitely attributable to police firing: the remainder may have been caused by military personnel on vehicles who, it is known, had, on occasion, to shoot their way out of roadblocks. *179 members of the public were treated in hospital for injuries caused by gunshot wounds, lathi blows or brickbats.*
Both on the side of the forces of law and order and on the side of the rioters there were doubtless many minor injuries which did not come to notice.

7. The result of the Commissioner's inquiries has been, in all cases but one, explicitly to exonerate the police from blame as regards opening fire and the quantum of firing that took place. In almost every case firing was resorted to in defence of life or of Government property. In the one case in which the Commissioner's finding is less definite as to the control of the firing and its quantum, the evidence is being reviewed by my Chief Secretary. The Commissioner's report indicates very clearly that *a very grave degree of disorder prevailed, especially in South Calcutta, for thrity-six hours on the 22nd and 23rd November* and while there may be reason to doubt (and this is a matter we are inquiring into) whether all the forces at the disposal of the C.P. were adequately utilised, there can be no doubt that the *forces actually employed were always hopelessly outnumbered, and*

often in a very tight corner in the face of an unusually determined and fanatical mob.

8. We have tried to draw for ourselves the necessary lessons from the events of these three hectic days. I think the first lesson is that, though the disturbances were not planned, at all events on the scale on which they took place, *there is a spirit of lawlessness abroad which, as in 1942, can, on a slight and sudden cause, be worked up with remarkable speed to produce, over a very wide area simultaneously, manifestations paralysing to the life of the community.* It is clear also that with every one of these outbreaks, *the technique of the mob is improving;* this was noticeable also in the methods of temporary sabotage indulged in by the water-works staff in the unconnected but simultaneous Corporation employees' strike.

This is a feature that may be expected to be even more marked in future disturbances, with the return to India of persons trained in sabotage, like the members of the I.N.A.

9. As I have already indicated, we are looking into the question whether the present system of employing sergeants as a striking force and keeping the Armed Police in reserve is that best calculated to produce satisfactory results.

10. Another lesson is that our Police transport was found to be in bad shape. We are replacing a considerable number of vehicles.

11. Of one thing we are all convinced—inter-communication between Police forces, police stations and outposts and police headquarters must be greatly improved, preferably by wireless. This applies both to Calcutta and to the Province

as a whole, and we are in course of making the necessary improvements and innovations in our communications.

12. So far as the mofussil is concerned, air transport may well exercise a determining force in nipping trouble in the bud. Thanks to the war, we already have a number of good aerodromes: we are examining urgently the provision of further airstrips to permit of quick reinforcement of our police in any district of the Province.
A problem to be faced will be that of keeping these landing grounds clear of deliberate obstruction when they are needed.

13. I am sending copies of this letter to the Governors of Bihar, Orissa and Assam.

I am, yours sincerely, R. G CASEY

V. SIR B. GLANCY (PUNJAB) TO FIELD MARSHAL VISCOUNT WAVELL (EXTRACT)

16 JANUARY 1946
SECRET

Relations between the different communities are getting more and more strained. The Deputy Commissioner of Ambala writes that "increasing reports of a deterioration in the communal situation, consequent on the poisonous propaganda of political parties, especially of the Muslim League, are being received from rural areas.

One very objectionable type of propaganda indulged in by the Muslim League is to threaten Muslim voters with excommunication including a refusal to allow their dead to be buried in Muslim graveyards and to debar them from joining in mass Muslim prayers in the event of their voting against the League." Much the same thing is happening in Lahore and other places.

Cries of "Jai Hind" are greeted with shouts of "Pakistan." The *conclusion of the first I.N.A. trial and the arrival of the three "heroes" in Lahore gave rise to a continual orgy of extravagant welcomes, speeches and entertainments.* The Congress Press has been full of jubilations. *One disturbing feature is the attendance of Indian Army personnel in uniform at meetings held in honour of the I.N.A. accused.*

A prominent Hindu, who is in close touch with the defence counsel, tells me that the most which they expected by way of commutation was that the sentence would be reduced to five years' imprisonment; I do not know to what extent this is true.

8

Intelligence Bureau's Report on INA Trials

The 1857 mutiny had thoroughly shaken the British empire in India. They were terrified of the spectre of such large-scale violence re-emerging in India. They strove their utmost thereafter to prevent the various castes, creeds and ethnicities of India from coming together again to stage another revolt. They sought to exploit every faultline in India whether of caste, creed or religion and language.

In 1887, Maj Gen Charles MacGregor was appointed QMG and head of Intelligence Department of the British Indian Army at Simla. Its task largely was to monitor the Russian troop deployments in Afghanistan. On December 23, 1887 the Intelligence Bureau (IB) was formed in India by the British Secretary of State. By the turn of the century the British were getting thoroughly alarmed with the rise of violent Indian revolutionary activities. In 1909, Indian Political Intelligence Office was established in London to counter the threat of Indian revolutionaries. The Indian Intelligence Bureau had in the meantime become one of the most efficient and effective Counter-Intelligence organisations in the world. It was successfully able to penetrate most of the Ghadr revolutionary cells being set up by Indian revolutionaries in the USA and England. All the revolutionary Indian plans to foment trouble in India during the First World War were ruthlessly foiled. There was no uprising whatsoever in India—even as 1.3 million Indian soldiers were sent to the various battlefields of the world. It was the result of a massive effort to divide and rule India and play off the various caste, creed, religious, ethnic and language groups against one another. India was kept thoroughly divided and Revolutionary groups kept under very effective watch and surveillance to ensure that India remained absolutely quiet and trouble free during the first Great War.

The success must be attributed to the Indian Intelligence Bureau which had become the most effective instruments of the Raj. In British Military intelligence circles there was a great deal of respect for the "India-wallas." Even more than the British Indian Army perhaps, the IB was the primary instrument to keep India under subjugation. The success of the IB in keeping India trouble free during the Great War made the British thoroughly arrogant and somewhat complacent. The Indians expected the British to be grateful after the War and perhaps grant Home Rule to India. What the Indians got instead was the racial arrogance of Jallianwala Bagh massacre in Punjab—the heartland from where the bulk of the Indian army was recruited. This generated a great wave of anger and indignation in India. It brought Mahatma Gandhi to the fore of the Indian independence movement. He changed the Congress party from an effete debating society of rich Indian lawyers to a mass-based, grass-roots movement that spread from the towns to the rural countryside. He started civil disobedience and escalated demands for home rule to *Poorna Svarajya*—or total independence. However his was a non- violent and peaceful movement. British political strategists and the Intelligence Bureau now felt that this non-violent movement was entirely manageable and the best bet for preventing the outbreak of large-scale violence as had happened in the Mutiny of 1857 (First War of Independence). So they tacitly encouraged Mahatma Gandhi and his brand of Non-violence over the violence of the revolutionaries.

By 1920 this had started to rise again. In 1921, The Indian Political Intelligence (IPI) was established as a state-run surveillance and monitoring agency. It was run jointly by the India Office and the Govt. of India. It reported jointly to the Secretary of Public and Judicial Department of the India Office and the Intelligence Bureau in India. All the attempts of Indian Revolutionaries to get arms support from Germany and Europe were foiled by the double agents of the IB in India. It was only the Japanese spree of conquest in South East Asia that shook the Raj and gave rise to a far more effective INA which now actualised the revolutionaries dreams and World War I era plans of invading India from the East. Bose was able to raise a 60,000-strong INA with the help of the Japanese Army and join their invasion of India in 1944.

The IB was at the forefront of the British campaign to destroy and subvert the INA. The IB thus was the most effective instrument of the Raj in suppressing all movements for Indian independence. Hence it is vital to see the IB report about the impact of the INA trials. This report from Director, Intelligence Bureau is most informative and telling as far as the impact of the INA is concerned. Even its measured and clinical tone gives a clear indication of the levels of disquiet. This report dated November 20, 1945 states inter alia that, "*Sardar Patel wanted the INA to be the nucleus of the new Indian Army.*" (It was Nehru who later, on Mountbatten's advice and pressure, refused to take the INA men back into the Indian Army and treated them as traitors. He stopped their pensions.) The report clearly highlights that "*the public feeling in India is one of sympathy and support for the INA. This sympathy is not confined to the towns but spreads to villages and across communities. It warns that this is likely to intensify. It warns clearly of the development of the agitation in dangerous directions and above all highlights that the threat to the security of the Indian Army is one which it would be unwise to Ignore.*"

The Director, Intelligence Bureau's Report of November 20, 1945 is reproduced below in full.

What is cause for considerable disquiet is the role of the Indian Intelligence Bureau immediately after the grant of independence. This organisation soon displaced the army and began to play a pivotal role in India's security decision making. Over time it completely marginalised the Armed Forces from any role in national security decision making. Worse, some of its senior officials seemed to retain a residual loyalty to the Raj. Institutional mechanisms were established to maintain links with the British MI5 via a liason office in New Delhi. Amazingly the IB continued to report to London about the activities of the relatives of Bose and ex-INA personnel till late into the 1960s. This raises some serious questions about the residual loyalties of some of the senior IB Officers and bureaucrats of that era. Tragically in more ways than one, it was not so much the Indian Army that was the last bastion of the Raj but sections of its highly competent and effective IB that retained residual loyalties to the Raj. The Intelligence agencies seem to have freed themselves of these colonial apron strings only by the decade of 1970 when India truly asserted its independence and autonomy and acted aggressively to shape outcomes in South Asia. In this the newly created R&AW under R. N. Kao played a stellar role. Let us now analyse the report of the Director, Intelligence Bureau in India dated November 20, 1945 that analyses the impact of the INA trials on the internal security scenario in India.

Intelligence Bureau's (Government of India, Home Department) Report on I.N.A. Trials

The report is given here as it appeared in "Transfer of Power," Volume 6, page 512.

Government of India, Home Department to the Secretary, Political Department, India office

New Delhi, 20th November 1945

Sir,

I am directed to forward for information a copy of a note prepared by the Director, Intelligence Bureau, on the I.N.A. situation.

I have the honour to be,

Sir,

Your most obedient servant,

F.G. Cracknell,

Deputy Secretary to the Govt of India

Enclosure

Secret

Intelligence Bureau

Home Department

The situation in respect of the Indian National Army is one which warrants disquiet. There has seldom been a matter which has attracted so much Indian public interest and, it is safe to say, sympathy.

Public feeling is based on political, racial, and sentimental considerations and has been influenced in a very great extent by the Press and platform writings and speeches of political leaders and organisations. The general Nationalist Press is completely in accord with political outcry and the effect the publications in question have is undoubted, for many of them are most popular and widely read even in rural areas. *The general line of the nationalist case is that the men of the I.N. A. were actuated by patriotic motives and the demand is made that none shall be punished. If there is punishment the result attending it will be racial bitterness which will last down through the ages.* The combined emphasis of current propaganda is on the treason aspect of the cases and other crimes are ignored. The way of propagandists is made easier because they have no counteracting propaganda with which to contend, and it is difficult to conceive now that counter effort could be effective in circumstances in which the country's ear has largely been captured. Congress has led this outcry since its commencement and continues to do so.

Whatever the motives of Congress may be, there is no doubt of the vast importance which is given to the subject in Congress's estimation and there is nothing to suggest that Congress might minimise its efforts or be delivered in any degree from the course it has adopted without complete Governmental acceptance of the demands put forward.

On the contrary there is every indication that Congress will use all the means available to it to create a still greater countrywide demand and inflame public opinion and that it will contribute it will continue to pursue this line determinedly throughout the election period and beyond and until events have exhausted their course. The fact that election propaganda is now in progress provides a convenient platform and growing audiences.

At most of the 160 political meetings held in the Central province during the first half of October demands were made for the abandonment of action against I.N.A. Similar demands were made at many meetings in other provinces. The number of meetings being held all over the country is now increasing.

Other political parties have followed Congress's lead some of them with marked determination and this can be said of *the Sikhs and the Hindu Mahasabha.* The influence of the Sikhs on the Central Punjab rural recruiting areas is great and daily meetings are being held by them at which demands on behalf of the I.N.A. are voiced. The Hindu Mahasabha lacks the rural influence of the Sikhs but their observance of an I.N.A. Day and their strongly worded appeals have had effect.

The Muslim League is in the forum with others but in the case of this organisation there is some reason to believe that as a party it is moved by considerations of expediency. However, the trial of Muslims may make their effect increasingly felt on the Muslim public and League alike.

Reports recently received have stated that growing enthusiasm is obvious at the meetings held in connection with I.N.A. Weeks and I.N.A. Days and that this is not only true of the towns but also of the villages. It was recently said about politicians active in their election campaigns that they had to speak of the I.N.A. in appreciative terms to interest their audiences. This was attributed partly to a wave of anti-British feeling which is now being deliberately fostered, partly to a genuine sympathy for the I.N.A. and partly to the fact that Army men on leave from Assam and Burma had not troubled enough to make their feelings known.
The source from which this information came also mentioned that there was surprise that speakers were being permitted so much licence by Government and that has been followed by the feelings that tongues could now wag with impunity.
That so much can be said without retribution has had a bad effect on those who might otherwise have supported the Government openly but now feel that silence is their best policy.

One thing seems clear and that is that sympathy for the I.N.A. is not the monopoly of those who are ordinarily against Government.
It is equally clear that this particular brand of sympathy cuts across communal barriers. This is explained to some extent by the fact that the thousands in the I.N.A. have many thousand relations who are anxious about their fate. There is, therefore, support for the political bodies who are helping the I.N.A. and a growing general bitterness. In many cases officers of the I.N.A. belong to influential families and this creates much local interest. If the families concerned do have traditions of loyalty, which is usually the case, the interest shown is intensified and also the ill-effects that attend it.

There is already evidence of some rather surprising approaches being made to Congress for assistance and the fact of ex-judge of the High Courts and gentlemen with titles joining openly in the defence of cases in which wartime treason is the charge is not negligible.

In reports received any public appreciation of Government's need to act and punish is hardly ever seen.
So far the campaign in favour of the I.N.A. has not resulted in any overt action against the Indian Army men or Europeans. In respect of the former there has been no hint of social boycott or anything of the of the kind and it may be that nothing of that character is intended.

The appearance of threatening posters, however, does not make the position in respect of Europeans as satisfactory as could be wished. Some respect for anonymous warning of this character has resulted from experience gained in earlier terrorist movements in India. Recently posters have appeared in Lahore and Calcutta and in the latter place were particularly objectionable. At this stage, however, it is unnecessary to take the matter of the posters too seriously.

Mention has already been made in this note of an opinion expressed that heretofore Army men on leave have not really made their views known with as much force as they could have used.
There have been numerous reports from Army sources that Army personnel and particularly returned prisoners of war feel very bitterly about the attitude the country and its politicians have adopted and that their animosity towards the I.N.A. is deep-seated. Intelligence so far received does not show that the influence of returned prisoners of war may not have returned in sufficient numbers yet to make their presence felt. In this connexion, however, it seems desirable to remember that serving men have also relation in the I.N.A. which may affect them in some degree.

At the same time, with "Blacks" and "Greys" being enlarged in large numbers they are not going to have the village field all to themselves. Indeed the former will have the advantage in some respects for many of *them will remain in their villages permanently and not temporarily as is the case with serving personnel. Meanwhile, there have been one or two newspaper reports of military clerical staff and men of the R. I. A. F. giving donations to defence funds.* On the whole, the speeches of nationalist leaders on the subject of the I.N.A. give the impression that careful thought has been given to wording and if they have any plans involving I.N.A., men in future they have avoided publicising them which is but prudent.

However, it is interesting in this connexion to note that is certain of his speeches in Bombay, *Patel has declared that what Government ought to do the I.N.A is to make it the nucleus of the new Indian Army,* which may be an indication of the lines on which his mind is travelling.

At the same time, Nehru, who has publicly referred to I.N.A. personnel as instructors in volunteer bodies. A more definite indication of a move in an unwarranted direction is contained in a recent report which alleges *that a Sabha is being formed in the north of India with the object of making contact with released I.N.A. officers and men in order to enrol them as members and educate and train them in the expectation that they will be of use to Congress* in its day-to-day activities and in the time of emergency. Even if the information is correct it may be that the inspiration to act on these lines is local in character. It is clear, however, that dangerous possibilities exist which merit very careful attention.

In summing up there seems justifications for attempting that:

(1) *The public feeling which exists is one of sympathy for the I.N.A.*
and genuine disapproval of its conduct is lacking.

(2) *The measure of sympathy is substantial and is not confined to towns or to any particular community, and that day by day it is being whipped up by the speeches of the nationalist leaders and the writings of the nationalist Press. This is likely to continue and intensify.*_

(3) In the absence of counter propaganda the nationalist campaign is having matters its own way, and that counter propaganda would be of doubtful value at this stage.

(4) *The possibility of the development of the agitation in dangerous directions exists in a degree which demands constant watchfulness*, and

(5) *The threat to the security of the Indian Army is one which it would be unwise to ignore.*

9

Endgame in London

The cumulative impact of the violent backlash to the INA trials in November-December 1945 and then the outbreak of mutinies in the Royal Indian Navy and some units of the Army at Jabalpur in February 1946 forced the British leadership to grant Independence to India. The crucial tipping point was the INA trials that unleashed such a spate of violence that the British high command in India totally lost its nerve. Their fears were not unjustified. Two and a half million battle-hardened Indian soldiers were being demobilised after the war. They now had a strong cadre of Indian officers to provide them leadership. The thoughtless British racial slurs had now proved very costly for the Raj. An objective analysis of the wealth of data and documentation available in "The Transfer of Power" archives in London provides more than ample evidence to support this thesis. Dr De has rendered yeoman service in scrutinising these archives of the Transfer of Power and putting the relevant documents together in his most excellent and telling monograph, "Netaji Subhash Chandra Bose: The Liberator of Indian Sub- continent." There is a starkly clear and visible paper trail that our historians now need to study and ingest. The pity is that this was available all along and has been so deliberately ignored and sidelined. This smacks of a deliberate attempt to falsify history and construct a false and contrived narrative designed to flatter the Raj and glorify the Anglophile Indians they had handed power to in India.

Just before independence, India had at the helm two highly experienced Soldiers who knew the British Indian Army very well—Lord Wavell the Viceroy and Fd Mshl Claude Auchinleck, the then Commander-in-Chief. The stream of reports they received from the ground—from the British Indian Army units and formations as also from the IB and the Governors of the Provinces about the intensity of feelings and unrest in the wake of the INA trials—convinced them that it was time to quit. The imperialists in London however were not convinced initially. Though the Labour Party had won the elections, they were in absolutely no mood to grant independence. This is crystal clear from documentary evidence. In fact in 1942, as the officiating Prime Minister, Clement Attlee himself had passed the orders to arrest all Congress leaders and crush the Quit India Movement ruthlessly. The stream of grim reports from New Delhi however soon disabused them of these fancy imperialist notions. The Post INA riots were unprecedented. Even when fired upon, the inflamed crowds were holding their ground, wavering just a little and then simply resuming the attacks. The IB informed them of the widespread sympathy and support for the men of the INA. The State Governors told them how these feelings cut across rural and urban settings and across community and creed faultlines. Above all it was the ominous and sullen mood building up in the army that was unnerving. Even as the imperialists in London continued to hang on to their tottering empire, Lord Wavell, who now understood the ground situation so very well, had virtually to give an ultimatum to London. Announce a firm timeline for quitting otherwise we can no longer hold on in India. Let's do it before we lose the power to control events. He went to the extent of daring the decision makers in London to remove him as Viceroy if they would not heed his advice. We have clearly seen this in Wavell's correspondence cited earlier in Chapter Six. In this chapter we see the grudging response from London—acknowledging the reality but then shooting the messenger. Lord Wavell was given his marching orders but his successor Lord Mountbatten was given a simple brief—get us out of India the smoothest way. Try and safeguard our interests as best as you can. Mountbatten and his wife did that brilliantly by playing upon Nehru's sentiments.

In this chapter we reproduce the documents emanating from the highest quarters in London—throwing in the towel but trying to keep this decision a closely guarded secret. Lord Wavell was asked to share this with his Commander-in-Chief and political advisor only but just orally. He was simply to show them the letter and it was not to be disseminated further. The empire had capitulated but wanted to keep this a tightly guarded secret and give the appearance of business as usual even as Mountbatten was sent with a clear brief—get us out of there as quickly as possible.

Wavell and Auchinleck felt they had at best 18 months— till mid-1948 in which to do it. Mountbatten advanced that to August 1947—he got the British out even faster. In the unseemly hurry to get out, he had some 14.5 million people displaced and 2 million killed in the Holocaust of Partition. The sum and substance of the correspondence cited in this chapter is simple—OK, do it, but don't let the natives know we are getting out.

The Tipping Point

From a perusal of the documents in the transfer of power archives, it is amply clear that the tipping point in India came with the INA trials and the outburst of popular emotions in its wake in November 1945 itself. The tipping point in London however came with the Mutiny in the Royal Indian Navy on February 18, 1946. The Raj needed this actual revolt to see the writing on the wall. Its officials in New Delhi had been sounding dire warnings but the leadership in London was loathe to listen to them till the roof caved in and 20,000 sailors of the Royal Indian Navy actually revolted, and shots were traded in Mumbai and Karachi and the sailors marched in the streets with photos of Netaji, shouting "Jai Hind." *The very next day on February 19, 1946, Lord Pethick-Lawrence made a momentous declaration in the House of Lords (just a day after the start of the naval mutiny) in which he announced the decision of the British government to send a special mission, consisting of himself, Sir Stafford Cripps and A. V. Alexander to resolve the constitutional deadlock in India. This was the beginning of the end, the final nail in the coffin of the empire.*

Very curiously, whom did the British commandeer to douse the flames of this revolt? The Congress party of course! They were now anxiously waiting on the sidelines to get the power for which they had been salivating for decades. When the revolt against the Empire actually broke out, it was the Congress leadership (Nehru and Patel, in particular) which collaborated with the Raj to douse the real flames of rebellion and cajoled the leaders of the Naval mutiny to surrender. In hindsight it appears their aim was less a hasty British exit but to ensure that they stepped into the very comfortable shoes of the Raj. The Whites would go but the Brown Sahibs would replace them and they needed the instruments the Raj had created. Nehru was so fond of Mountbatten and his wife, that he retained him for another two years as the first Governor General of the Dominion of India (even as the new born Dominion of Pakistan opted for one of its own—Mohammad Ali Jinnah—a pork eating, born-again Muslim, to be its first Governor General).

"The King is dead, long live the King"—that seemed sadly to be the sum and substance of it all in India. The British did leave finally but left behind their loyal minions who would zealously safeguard the legacy of the Raj and the narratives of imperial justice it had created to justify its exploitative rule. The British left in an atmosphere of total bonhomie. They had placed people in power who would ensure them a warm send-off for looting the people of India for 200 years and more. So loyal would the Congress under Nehru remain to the legacy of the Raj that it would treat the INA men as traitors, refuse to take them back into the army and kept tabs on the relatives of Subhash Bose and keep reporting on them to the MI5 in London. Above all it would strive to declare Bose as dead even as it perhaps had information that he was in a Siberian prison cell undergoing torture and privation.

In this chapter therefore we record the endgame of the empire as it most reluctantly took the decision to leave but kept it a well-guarded secret even as it began to implement the process for quitting India. The task was given to a flamboyant and vainglorious new Viceroy, Lord Louis Mountbatten. His charming wife went out of the way to befriend Nehru and clearly influenced him into safeguarding the legacy of the Raj. The paper trail in London documents the demise of the Raj in these letters that were then an ultra secret. One is quoting directly from the transfer of power archives in London. The top leadership in London wanted the decision to quit India finally to be kept as a very closely guarded secret. The empire had caved in but was loathe to admit the same publicly to the natives. It was a most grudging decision precipitated not by Gandhi's non-violent movement and Satyagraha but as this voluminous documentary evidence clearly reveals, by the rather violent riots that broke out in the wake of the INA trials and finally the mutiny in the Royal Indian Navy was the last straw that broke the camel's back in London

THE BRITISH RAJ IN LONDON DECIDES TO GRANT INDIA'S INDEPENDENCE

The reports on the decision-making process are given here as they appeared in "Transfer of Power," Volume 6, pages 1106,

1107, 1108.

I. LORD PETHICK-LAWRENCE TO MR. ATTLEE

INDIA OFFICE

4 March 1946

TOP SECRET

Secretary of State's Minute

Prime Minister

I attach copies of the telegrams sent to the Viceroy after the Chequers meeting and of two telegrams received from him in reply last night. I propose to discuss the terms of the answer to be sent to these telegrams with Cripps and Alexander and will send the draft
of what we propose for your consideration. I hope to be able to do this on Wednesday. There is, however, one immediate point for decision.
The Viceroy asks to be allowed to show the draft Directive to the Commander-in-Chief, the Home Member, the Political Adviser and the Reforms Commissioner. In telegram 5-U he refers to the necessity for consulting the Commander-in-Chief and the Political Adviser.
If you agree I would propose to tell the Viceroy that we do not wish the Directive to be disclosed to as many people as he
suggests but that we agree to his consulting the Commander-in-Chief and the Political Adviser orally. I should make it clear that, while he may show them the document, they should not be given copies.

As regards what the Viceroy says about the Defence provision.
I have asked for the opinion of the Chiefs of Staff as to what Defence provision they consider it essential to ensure in a settlement of the Indian question.

PETHICK-LAWRENCE

II. LORD PETHICK-LAWRENCE TO MR. ATTLEE INDIA OFFICE

4 March 1946

TOP SECRET

Secretary of State's Minute

Prime Minister

The King wishes to see the Ministers who are going to (given in next page).
On 5 March Mr. Attlee noted: "I agree with this Minute."

The King wishes to see the Ministers who are going to India and we shall have an audience with him shortly. I think I heard you tell Sir Stafford Cripps that *you had spoken to the King but I do not know how much you have told him orally of our plans in regard to India.*

Clearly, however, he ought to be informed *that we are prepared to contemplate a settlement on the basis that India will not remain within the Empire, and as this will affect the King's title I presume that his approval is necessary*.

If you have not already told him I imagine you will wish to inform him yourself before our audience, the time of which was fixed for Friday next at noon but may be postponed owing to the Cabinet I should be glad to have a note of what you have said or written to him to guide myself and my colleagues at our audience. I presume that a formal written approval by the King will not be necessary until a later stage.

PETHICK-LAWRENCE

III. LORD PETHICK-LAWRENCE TO FIELD MARSHAL VISCOUNT WAVELL INDIA OFFICE

5 March 1946 3.50 pm

IMMEDIATE

The directive is intended to be Cabinet instruction to Ministers & yourself. It is being restricted to very narrow circle here and I fear we cannot agree to as wide a disclosure of it as you propose.

We agree however to your consulting C. in C & Political Adviser personally on the understanding that they are shown the text but are not given copies.

IV. MINUTE BY MR. ATTLEE

10 DOWNING STREET, WHITEHALL,

5 March 1946

I told him that the basis of our negotiations was necessarily based on the Cripps offer which gave India the freedom to choose her future, which might be independence.

He did not dissent from this.

C. R. A.

* * *

The British Prime Minister Mr. Attlee agreed to the Secretary of State's Minute, which proposed India's Freedom, the Viceroy Field Marshal Viscount Wavell and the Commander-in-Chief General Sir

Claude Auchinleck were informed, and finally King George VI did not dissent.

Thus, the trials of the I.N.A. officers Shah Nawaz Khan, Prem Kumar Sehgal, Gurbaksh Singh Dhillon and others at Red Fort in Delhi eventually brought the end of the British Raj in the Indian Subcontinent.

But before the Raj declared it, the British Administration proceeded towards the processes of dividing the country based on religious issue and then declared the subcontinent's Freedom.

Thus, the countries in the Indian subcontinent got their Independence. (King George VI)

10

A Summation: Rectifying History

The purpose of this book was to examine precisely how the post-colonial regime emerged in India. A deliberate narrative has been woven around our freedom struggle to carefully censor out any role of violence in what is deliberately packaged and sold as a unique, one of its kind, freedom struggle based on non-violence, ahimsa and the psychological pressure methodology advocated by Mahatma Gandhi. He had begun this mode of civil disobedience and mass protest in South Africa. It was later followed there by Nelson Mandela. We forget to notice one sad fact. Despite following Gandhis non-violent struggle methods, South Africa became free only in April 1994—almost towards the close of the twentieth century. Had India stuck to non-violence alone, there is a good chance that we would have received our freedom around the same time, if at all.

The simple fact I have tried to establish in this book is that the final charge of Mahtma Gandhi's non-violent movement had failed dismally in 1942 and after that the Congress was largely a spent force. The new Labour Government in London was as determined as the Conservatives not to grant independence to India. Lord Clement Attlee, in fact had jailed the entire Congress leadership in 1942. So what changed so suddenly? How and why did India, and other Asian states, obtain their freedom from 1947 onwards? The answer is simple. The British empire in Asia was fatally wounded by its violent military struggle with Nazi Germany and Japan. It was particularly the war with Japan in South East Asia that had really uprooted the Empire as it suffered humiliating defeats in one country after another. In virtually under a year, the British empire had been rolled out of Malaya, Singapore and Burma. The military defeat of the White colonial power at the hands of an Asian military, broke that myth of military invincibility of the empire and the white races. The surrendering British officers simply abandoned their men to the Japanese. Major Fujiwara, the Japanese Lawrence of Arabia as it were, helped raise the first INA from Indian prisoners of war with the help of Manmohan Singh.

Meanwhile in India, Subhash Bose had clearly seen that World War II provided a golden , once-in-a-lifetime opportunity for India to gain its freedom. There is a lot of moralising that he took the help of the genocidal Nazi power in Germany and Imperial Japan. The simple fact is that he was being an absolute realist who realised the truth of the Kautilyan dictum—an enemy's enemy is my friend. He realised that it was futile to expect British gratitude by assisting their war effort. At the end of World War I, the British attitude was one of crude racial superiority. The Indians were then expecting gratitude for their services during the War, where some 80,000 Indians had laid down their lives. What they got instead was a massacre. It had resulted in the Jallianwala Bagh massacre in the prime recruiting area of the British Indian Army that had contributed so much in that war. Indian expectations of gratitude after the Second World War were as misplaced. In fact, Churchill was on record to state that any assurances given to the Indians during the Second World War need not be honoured after it was over.

Bose had correctly identified the loyalty of the native Indian sepoy to the Raj as its real centre of gravity. If this could be shaken, the Raj would not last a day. The *British colonial enterprise had succeeded so brilliantly in India as a result of the success of their Nativisation drive.* They were able to raise a vast army of local native sepoys, trained on modern European lines and led by British officers. It was with these native Indian army of sepoys that they had conquered and ruled India for over two hundred years. At any given time in India, the British white troops hardly numbered more than 40,000. The Indian sepoys were 150,000 in number before the war. In World War I the British Indian Army was rapidly expanded to 1.3 million. In World War II it was raised to an all-time record level of 2.5 million men—the largest all-volunteer army in the history of the world. The British, however, could rule only as long as the native sepoys remained loyal to the Raj. Bose had clearly understood this. In Germany he had raised the Indische Legion from the Indian prisoners of war. As the tide of war turned he realised that he had been stuck in the wrong theatre. The Japanese now began to ask for Bose as British efforts at subversion had caused problems in the first INA.

Bose was now sent by submarine to South East Asia. It was the only case of submarine to submarine transfer in the Second World War. Bose now took charge of the INA and expanded it to three divisions worth—some 60,000 men. He established a Free India Government-in-exile in Singapore in October 1943. It was recognised by 11 countries—including the Soviet Union. He declared war on the British and Americans. He joined the Japanese invasion of India in 1944. Unfortunately, by then the tide of the war had turned fully with the entry of America on the side of the Allies. It was too little, too late. Had the same attack come in 1942, or even 1943, it would have gone like a knife through butter. Bose was certain that the moment the news of the INA on Indian soil reached the Indian people, it would galvanise them magically and cause an uprising. Unfortunately, the British wartime censorship kept the INA one of the best secrets of the war. After the war the British acted with typical racial arrogance. In a very foolish gesture of triumphalism designed to overawe the natives, they carried out highly publicised trials of three INA officers at the iconic Red Fort in New Delhi. The news of the INA now tumbled out of the wartime closet. As Bose had predicted so accurately, it galvanised the nation, and caused a nationwide uprising. The very knowledge of the INA—an army of dedicated Indians fighting and dying to free India—was enough to put the towns and countryside on fire. The very racial arrogance of this gesture inflamed the people of India. It hit at the very centre of gravity of the Raj and forever changed the loyalty of the Indian soldier. The British were exhausted and war-weary after six years of bloodletting. Their armies were desperately homesick and war-weary and in no mood now to fight 2.5 million Indian soldiers who had done so well on the various battlefields of the Second World War.

Wavell and Auchinleck realised that the loyalty of the Indian sepoy to the Raj was now a major question mark. It was all over for the Raj. They rightly advised London that the British should cut their losses and leave with grace. This was not accepted initially by the imperialists in London. However, by February 1946 mutinies had actually broken out in the Royal Indian Navy and some units of the army. The Raj in London now saw the dire warnings of their Viceroy and Commander-in-Chief in India coming true and actualising before their very eyes. They threw in the towel and decided to quit. Mountbatten was sent in to oversee the process of extrication and the winding up of the empire. So, in the end, it was old-fashioned violence, and the threat of it on an even greater scale, that resulted in a withdrawal of British power from South Asia. Despite whatever romantic illusions that have been created by court historians, non-violence and soft power had little to contribute to nation-state formation in post-colonial India.

Summary of Findings

In this book, we have examined this hypothesis in a very logical and academically rigorous format. We first identified the key decision makers of the British Empire. We then examined the voluminous details available in the now declassified Transfer of Power archives in London. The entire documentary trail of evidence has been very well preserved for posterity. A clinical and empirical examination of the voluminous documentary evidence clearly highlights the failure of the non-violent movement and the overwhelming impact of the INA trials and subsequent mutinies on the British decision to quit. Without the INA trials and the subsequent large-scale violence and actual mutinies, there was simply no question of the British leaving when they did. As stated, we identified the key British decision makers as:

- Prime Minister Lord Clement Attlee who was then also the Defence Minister. He was the critical and overall the key decision maker. So far there was only a second or third-hand report of what he had said in private to Justice P. B. Chakraborty, the acting Governor of West Bengal in 1956. Now we have examined a whole body of his correspondence during that critical period, which has been duly preserved in the Transfer of Power archives in London. We now have clear primary evidence and an authentic paper trail that unravels the entire mystery and lays bare the essentials of the British process of decision making. This is solid documentary evidence that needs now to be meticulously analysed. This clinching evidence leaves no scope for doubt at all and conclusively establishes my thesis that it was primarily the INA trials that precipitated the British withdrawal.
- Other two key decision makers in London were Secretary of State for India and Burma Lord Pethick-Lawrence and to a lesser extent Lord G. H. Hall, Secretary of State for Colonies. *The Secretary of State, Lord Pethick-Lawrence, did not initially agree with Wavell's appreciation. He felt that it was still possible to hold on to India, and proposed further European recruitment to augment British troops in India.* His gratuitous advice was, however, rapidly overtaken by events.
- The key Decision makers in India were of course the two highly experienced India hands—Lord Wavell the Viceroy and Fd Mshl Claude Auchinleck, the Commander-in-Chief. Their written reports and above all the clinical military Appreciation

of the Situation by Auchinleck in end November 1945, provide clinching and overriding documentary evidence of the massive psychological impact of the INA trials on the final British decision to quit. Their written reports constitute the most clinching proof of the overwhelming impact of the INA on the British decision to Quit.

- The reports of the Governors of the Provinces provide clinching evidence of the overwhelming impact of these INA trials in the various parts of India. All the Governors were unanimous that the impact cut across caste and community lines, across urban and rural terrains and was all-India in character and impact. They have all echoed that the reliability of Indian troops to act against their own people, was now a serious question mark. Casey of Bengal graphically described how mobs in Calcutta were not deterred by small arms fire but when fired upon, just wavered a bit and then moved on to resume the attack.
- Lastly we have the clinical and objective report of the Director of Intelligence (IB) in the wake of the INA trials. In a measured and understated tone, it sets out clearly that the post INA trials situation had created a serious internal security problem and highlights that its impact on the Indian Army simply could not be ignored. The INA was growing more popular by the day and any action against them would lead to serious consequences. Indian serving soldiers in uniform were attending meetings to felicitate the returning INA soldiers who were now being universally treated as national heroes.
- To this exhaustive list we need to add the Military Intelligence reports of the Army. These were personally seen by Lt Gen S. N. Sinha, who was the first Indian Officer to be posted to the Military Operations Directorate in 1947. This was, till then, the exclusive preserve of white British officers only. The Director, Military Intelligence had clearly concluded in 1945 that Indian troops could no longer be relied upon to act against their own countrymen. Gen Sinha had also seen the Contingency plans for

flying and shipping in five divisions worth of White troops in case of large-scale mutinies and Op Gandola, the plan to evacuate all white military and civilian personnel and their families in case of a general uprising. These are all indicative of a general air of alarm and panic and foreboding about what was to come. These clearly highlight the massive and decisive psychological impact of the INA and Bose on the British decision makers.

The Role of Mahatma Gandhi

What then was the role of Mahatma Gandhi in the British decision to quit India? Much depends upon how this question is framed. Justice P. B. Chakraborty had framed this question in rather straightforward terms to Lord Clement Attlee in 1956. He had contextualised it in terms of the abject failure of the Quit India Movement in 1942. Why then did the British have to leave in such a tearing hurry in 1947? Attlee had answered truthfully that it was the violence generated by the INA trials as also the impact it had on the loyalty of the native Indian troops, and the mutinies in the Royal Indian Navy, etc., which forced the British to leave. As a legal luminary, the Chief Justice persisted and asked another blunt question—what, then, was Mahatma Gandhi's non-violent movement's role in the British decision to quit. Attlee's cryptic and sarcastic response is now famous all over the social media—he said Attlee's face twisted in a sarcastic smile as he spelt out the word "minimal."

It is an emphatic and clear-cut response. The only problem is the secondary/tertiary nature of this evidence. Justice Chakraborty told this to R. C. Majumdar the historian, about what Attlee had said to him. As such the absolute veracity of this statement could be questioned by sceptical scholars, though both interlocutors were men of unimpeachable integrity. This, however, could never amount to be the sole evidence to settle such a vital debate about the historic origins of the post-colonial state in India.

That is why in this book trouble has been taken to examine a whole body of documentary evidence contained in the declassified

Transfer of Power Archives. There is a wealth of material there, first-hand evidence that is clinching and incontrovertible and which settles this debate conclusively, once and for all.

However, in the interests of objectivity and fair play we may have to reframe the original question. *What was Mahatma Gandhi's role in the Freedom Struggle of India?* (This is different from questions about final outcome.) Here we can truthfully answer—a great deal. He was a saintly figure who metamorphosed the Congress from an effete debating club of rich lawyers petitioning the Queen on behalf of her uneducated Indian subjects, against the minions who ran her empire. Gandhi came at a critical turning point in the Freedom Struggle—the massacre of Jallianwala Bagh in (1919).

The British racial arrogance was at its peak then. The highly efficient Intelligence Bureau had foiled each and every violent revolutionary plot to overthrow the empire. India had been kept peaceful and incident free during the war even as 1.3 million troops had been sent out to fight the war in Europe, Middle East and Africa. There had been a fear that if the Indian army was taken out in substantial numbers, it could result in large-scale violence erupting in India. Nothing of that sort happened. Indian society had been most thoroughly divided on caste and creed lines and the very idea of India had been destroyed. There was therefore no need for the British to show any gratitude to the natives for their support during the war. The natives had no bloody choice and if they had any notions of a non-white people getting Dominion status, that would be ruthlessly extinguished.

Gandhi came upon the scene at this critical juncture. He studied the Indian situation and transformed the elitist Congress into a mass-based organisation that reached out to the grass-roots level in the villages of India where 70% of the Indian population lived. This mass mobilisation was a massive and impressive exercise that revived the idea of a grass-roots India that lived largely in her villages that were poor and impoverished. Gandhi realised that the Indians were in no position then to offer armed resistance. *So he made a virtue out of necessity and chose non-violence, non-cooperation and civil disobedience as his methods. He gave the largely Urban Indian freedom movement a rural and egalitarian bias.* Gandhi's movement attracted many brilliant and sincere Indians of that era—like Nehru, Azad, Patel and Bose. Unfortunately, even this non-violent struggle was carried out in fits and starts. Gandhi was very careful not to cross the British tolerance thresholds and he personally intervened to prevent this movement from turning violent. That was the failing of this mass movement. It could never generate cumulative pressure of an order that would force the Raj to capitulate.

British Manipulation of the Gandhian Movement

The pity is that the British strategists soon realised the non-decisive and the largely ineffectual nature of this non-violent movement. It could be disconcerting and disruptive but could never generate the sustained level of pressure that could unravel the empire. On the contrary it prevented the outbreak of large-scale violence. Gandhi himself would ensure that as he was genuinely wedded to non-violence. The British now very cleverly manipulated this mass movement by actually giving an inordinate media build-up to Mahatma Gandhi and his unique but ineffectual movement. This was a threat they could handle and as such they hugely preferred it over violent revolutionary movements which posed a very real danger to the Raj. *Ahinsa* kept the masses timid and non-violent. In that condition the Raj could deal with such a movement for decades, if not a century or more. In actual practice Nelson Mandela carried out precisely such a peaceful mass movement in South Africa. It took that country till April 1994 to get their freedom. In actual fact, the non-violent example actually delayed the onset of freedom in the European colonies in Africa.

It was Bose who saw this with astonishing clarity. The effete non-violent movement could continue forever without achieving any concrete results. It could sputter on ineffectually for decades.

The British success in India was one of Nativisation. They had used an Indian army of natives to establish and maintain their empire in India. The key centre of gravity of the empire was the loyalty of the native sepoy to the Raj. If this was subverted, the Raj would come to an immediate and inglorious end. Gandhi initially had Bose hounded out of the Congress for his rebellion. But Bose was right. The most opportune time for launching a violent liberation movement was the war itself. Britain now had powerful enemies prepared to help such a violent movement to emerge in India. The Japanese had given this serious thought and ultimately helped to create the INA. Just two years after driving Bose out, Gandhi veered very close to the views of Bose, especially as to timings. The saint could still not bring himself around to endorse his violent methods. Gandhi forced the Congress to launch the final Quit India Movement even while the war was on. Loyalists of the empire like Nehru and Azad differed with Gandhi but were overruled. The non-violent movement was snuffed out by the British who mobilised 57 white battalions to do this. The Congress leadership was rounded up and jailed and blanked out entirely from the print and radio media of that era using draconian wartime censorship of the news. In terms of timing, had the Japanese Army and the INA attacked then (in 1942-43) they would have made mincemeat of the empire in India.

For once the traditionally bold Japanese military hierarchy had lost its nerve and dithered fatally. When they did get down to attacking India in 1944, it was a classic case of too little, too late. The miracle is that despite the odds they almost pulled it off. The battles of Imphal-Kohima were one of the most bitterly fought battles of that war. But in the end it culminated in a major defeat and misery for the combined Japanese-INA forces. As we have seen, precisely as Bose had predicted , the INA lost the battles but won the war for Indian independence. We have seen in detail just how. The outcome of the Indian war for independence, Bose had said, would be independent of the outcome of the Second World

War. That was precisely how it came about. Bose thus proved to be one of the great strategic thinkers and practioners of that era. His insight was remarkable for its penetration into the essence of the problem and his anlaysis always proved to be objective and firmly rooted in reality. The solutions he advocated delivered concrete results.

Both Bose and Gandhi were highly charismatic leaders with a deep insight into the Indian psyche. *Gandhi was a great organiser who created an egalitarian, rural, mass-based movement for freedom in India. However in terms of achieving outcomes, this movement failed to deliver till Bose intervened and redirected it into the classical violent channels.* The modern nation state is premised upon the monopoly of violence and Bose created the instrumentalities for a violent overthrow of the empire in the form of the INA. Its use by itself galvanised India and awoke its dormant sense of self. It was Bose and his violent methods that ultimately liberated India in 1947 itself—just two years after the Second World War which the British had finally won. The war left Britain exhausted and spent and drained of the will to maintain its empire, especially in the face of massive armed rebellion. Bose's stellar contribution was to make that threat become very real and credible. The INA trials shook the empire in India. The mutinies that followed in February 1946 sounded the death knell of that empire. In the end, the same Armies that had subjugated the Indian people, helped to get them their freedom. Let us not forget it was the Indian army that had revolted in 1857 as also in 1946 (Royal Indian Navy). The pity was that the British succeeded in transferring power to their handpicked set of AngloPhile brown sahibs who remained beholden to the Raj for a good half century after the British had left.

The Nehruvian Narrative

The Congress party had elected Sardar Patel as the first Prime Minister of free India. However in a surprising act of wilfulness,

Gandhi ensured that the mantle was given to Nehru—an avowed Anglophile who was so very close to Mountbatten and his wife. Nehru clearly had a problem of political legitimacy. The voting had gone in Sardar Patel's favour. But even more than Patel, Nehru was wrestling with the Ghost of Bose. The whole nation knew that India had finally won its freedom only because of Bose and the INA, 26,000 of whom had laid down their lives. Such a scale of casualties hardly justified the fiction of an entirely non-violent movement for freedom. Both the departing British empire and the new Nehruvian dispensation, now worked energetically to craft a brand new narrative—India had won its freedom solely and only due to the non- violent Freedom Movement of the Nehru-Gandhi dispensation. Force or violence had simply no role to play in getting India her freedom. *The British empire also tom-tommed the fiction of a non-violent struggle so that the remaining colonies in Africa would emulate this brilliant new model. As a sad outcome, the freedom of the African colonies was inordinately delayed by a couple of decades.* The British Raj now acquired a new-found halo of liberalism and benevolence that masked its true exploitative and rapacious character.

Hence Nehru's political legitimacy stemmed from the fiction of this non-violent struggle. To support this fictional narrative, Nehru now put on the airs of a great Pacifist who abhorred war and violence and did not even want India to have an Army. He only needed the Police! Fortunately for India, the far more realistic Sardar Patel prevented Nehru from actualising his pacifist fancies. The tragedy was he passed away too soon. A whole host of court historians, like Bipin Chandra and the rest, were drafted to dismiss the role of Bose and his INA and claim all credit for India's freedom solely via the agency of a unique and one of its kind freedom struggle that was absolutely non-violent in character. The real leadership of this, one-of-a-kind freedom struggle, of course had come from Gandhi and Nehru alone and hence this family was now destined to rule India forever.

The sum and substance of this new narrative spelt out by Bipin Chandra and the Court Historians is as follows: *that because of the continual non-violent struggle of the Congress over the past several decades, a kind of momentum towards freedom had been built up and what was germane or critical, was simply_the process of negotiations, which Gandhi and Nehru seemed to lead.* So Bose and the INA had nothing to do with India getting her Freedom. it was a failed non- event, not even a footnote in the real Freedom Struggle led by Gandhi and Nehru that was entirely peaceful.

This thesis merits a specific examination and refutation. I would list the following points against it:

- The non-violent Freedom struggle had proceeded in fits and starts. Its peaks or spurts came in 1930 and 1942 with large gaps of inactivity in-between. Hence no sustained momentum was generated as alleged.
- The final, culmination point of this movement came in August 1942 when the British mobilised some 57 battalions of White troops to crush it decisively. The entire Congress leadership was jailed and nothing was heard thereafter of them till 1944 when the Japanese invasion had been repelled and they could be safely released.
- When Gandhi emerged from prison in 1944 he was largely a spent force and a man broken in health and spirit. He presented many legalistic arguments then to state that he was no longer in charge of the Congress and could take no decisions. He said he had no authority to start the civil disobedience movement and would support the war effort. He in fact asked his followers who had gone underground to come out of hiding. This was a sad admission of defeat and total capitulation.
- Churchill lost the elections immediately after the war. The Labour Government however had no intentions of giving up the empire. Lord Clement Attlee, the new Prime Minister had been officiating as PM for a while in 1942 in the wartime Coalition

Government, and had given orders for the vicious crackdown on the Quit India Movement and proscribing of the Congress and jailing of its entire top leadership. He was no bleeding-heart liberal, as far as the empire was concerned.

- Thus all the so-called "momentum towards Freedom" had clearly and completely petered out by the end of the War. The court historians are being less than objective and honest when they talk of the inexorable momentum built up by the long-winded non-violent movement.
- However, things changed suddenly and abruptly due to the INA trials which galvanised the whole of India. Serious disturbances broke out in the wake of these trials in November-December 1945. These greatly alarmed the British military and political leadership in India. Both Wavell and Auchinleck, seasoned India hands, realised the gravity of the change that had taken place. The Indian troops could no longer be counted upon to defend the tottering Raj. In their absence, the Raj just did not have adequate British troops to hold on to even the main towns and cities of India and the airports from which they could be flown out in an emergency of a widespread revolt. They asked that a clear-cut decision to Quit India be formulated and made known to all. In simple terms they asked the Raj to Quit with grace as it was now all over. Nativisation had now failed.
- The simple fact is that the imperialists in London initially did not agree with this apparently defeatist argument. The non-violent movement had put no such pressure on New Delhi or London. Even large-scale violent protests by the civilian population in the wake of the INA trials failed to move them sufficiently. Lord Pethick-Lawrence disagreed with Wavell and Auchinleck and asked for enrolment of European troops to hang on to India. it was a civilian's pipe dream and the soldiers rightly scoffed at it. How long would it take London to recruit and train this brand new army of European mercenaries to fight the beastly natives? From where in Europe would this Army of mercenaries be

recruited? Who would pay for them? The whole of Europe was devastated by the war and sick and tired of fighting then. The British troops themselves were drained and exhausted after six years of war and in no mood or shape to re-conquer India in the face of dogged resistance by the 2.5 million demobilised Indian soldiers. So the arguments of sustained pressure built up by the non-violent movement are simply and purely unteneble. Here was a Raj that was unwilling to capitulate even in the wake of widespread violence in India.

- The final tipping point in London came with the Naval Mutiny of February 1946. It clearly highlighted to London that their Generals on the ground in India were not imagining things and conjuring up horror scenarios that were unrealistic or alarmist. They were now struck by the cold water of harsh reality and they finally caved in. The Raj threw in the towel only after the naval mutiny.
- The great pity is that the Congress jumped in to douse the flames of this Naval mutiny. They were the self-styled great negotiators who felt that they had finally worn the British Raj down by their sheer oratory and negotiating skills! With all the details of the decision-making process in New Delhi and London from 1945 to 1947 now available, we can treat these self-serving estimates and highly exaggerated and insufficiently contextual claims with the contempt they deserve.
- The very sad part is how a set of self-serving court historians have blithely ignored a vast body of documentary evidence available in the Transfer of Power archives and how they have been allowed to go unchallenged so far. In this book we have presented that whole body of empirical and irrefutable evidence that was available all along. We have not just quoted selectively but reproduced the entire letters and correspondence for perusal and analysis. It is time now to rescue our history as a nation state from a self-seeking bunch of sycophants and shameless spin-doctors still faithfully serving the Raj and its successor dynasty.

- The arguments in this book are not emotive but empirical and based on primary and most authentic sources from the British archives. These have not just been cited but reproduced in their entirety. We have cited the correspondence and estimates of the key British decision makers of that era themselves to unravel the details of the process of decision making that led to India becoming free. The role of Bose and INA stands out as clear as daylight through this entire set of correspondence.

11

Epilogue: Nation State and Nationalism in India

I had stated at the outset of this book, that few nations in history have had their sense of self and identity as a civilisational nation state so comprehensively destroyed as India's was. Over two centuries, the British Colonial state undertook a highly effective campaign to exploit every faultline in India's body politic—to divide and rule, to abjectly divide India on the basis of caste and creed, religion, race and language. As Dr. Mithi Mukherjee writes: *"If the British Empire had to survive in India ... it had to destroy and dismantle all sources of Indian unity and identity—cultural, political and historical; and render the very idea of India as meaningless. ... Torn by internal conflict, it was claimed that India was in desperate need of a neutral and impartial power at the helm of the state to secure justice and order (or justice as order). Given that Indian society was deeply divided into communities in conflict with each other, only an alien, foreign power could be trusted to be neutral and impartial."*

What was worse was a concerted campaign to psychologically destroy the very idea of India and impose in the minds of the subject races a congenital sense of inferiority of civilisational values and culture. Everything Indian was now deemed as lowly and inferior by the victims of this concerted psychological warfare campaign, to make the natives feel low down and inferior. The victims of this mass programming of subject minds led them to deeply ingrain these colonial narratives. In fact Macaulay was recruited by the British to destroy the native Brahmanical based system of education and replace it with a Colonial model which would churn out loyal and devoted clerks, scribes and coolies for the empire. Everything *desi* or native was automatically deemed to be inferior to what industrialised Great Britain had to offer. This encompassed all fields—whether cultural, political and historical, or even in the realm of arts and crafts. India had no tradition of high art—Indians were just craftsmen who blindly followed archaic traditions and formulae by rote and could produce nothing creative or original. It was a civilisational assault of a scope and scale that has never been seen before. It virtually succeeded in destroying the very Indian identity and sense of self so very comprehensively that even 70 years after independence, Indians remain in thrall of those pernicious colonial narratives that are repeated by those brown sahib historians.

Thus Max Mueller was employed by the East India company to write the history of India for the natives and feed them a very deliberate set of Colonial narratives. The Aryan invasion theory was propagated by him—to justify the imposition of foreign rule in India. The Aryans themselves were invaders and foreigners in this land. How could they grudge the British the same privilege of invading and conquering India? They foisted racial constructs on Indian history by creating the myth of the White Aryan and Black Dravidian races—a North-South racial divide that is totally illusory and not borne out by empirical gene-mapping studies. North and South of the Vindhyas Indians share the same set of genes. The attack has been on the very idea of India. Ask most educated Indians today, and they will forcefully assert that there was no nation called India before 1947. Nationhood was a gift bestowed upon us by the British empire. In all history there was never an entity called an Indian nation, not even a civilisational state. The trenchant hold of colonialism and its narratives of inferiority of Indian culture is borne out by the fact that almost every Indian village today has an English-medium school where natives learn the English language to feel emancipated. The most trenchant colonial narrative that has been ingrained in the Indian mind is that India was never a nation state. Nation hood was imposted from outside by the empire. Thus India became a nation state only in 1947. It was never one earlier. It is this myth that we need to question in an empirical fashion. Hence it becomes essential to understand first what precisely is a nation and how does it become a nation state. That is the core myth of the colonial period that still has a trenchant hold upon the Indian imagination. The British claimed India was never a nation or even a civilizational state. It was a competing cauldron of castes and creeds forever at war amongst themselves. It needed an external agency to rule and provide justice and order to the competing castes and creeds.

In recent times, the leftist intellectuals have come up with bizarre notions about the very concept of nation state and nationalism. A nation state, as per them, is merely a collection of nationalities who are free to come and go as they please (as crowds move into and out of a railway platform). What then about the notions of territoriality and nativity that are central to the concept of a nation state? People are born into a nation state by virtue of the fact that they were born on its territory. Territory is sacred and nations fight wars to defend their boundaries. I am a citizen because I am born to parents who were in turn citizens of India—the aspect of nativity comes to the fore. Today the very concept of nation and nation state are being deliberately redefined to weaken large states like India. Hence, at the end of this book, it would be most essential to take a look at these very notions of nation state and nationalism as they relate specifically to India. Bose was an ardent nationalist and helped to crystallise the very idea of a strong nation state in India beyond the divisions of caste, creed and language. Today India is in dire need to revive its fading nationalism and inculcate the burning patriotism of Bose and his INA, into its citizens. The British colonial regime had propagated the belief that India was never a nation. This now needs to be analysed and refuted in detail.

Nationalism

There is a need to clearly understand what nationalism means and what it implies. Key to the existence of nation states are racial memories that are shared amongst the people who constitute that state. Thus, *every nation has its own understanding of its distinctive past that is conveyed through stories, myths and history. These stories and_myths may not be historically accurate. The key however is the trenchant strength of these shared beliefs.* So, whether historically accurate or otherwise, these memories contribute to the understanding of the present. It is this continuity of the narratives between the past and present that provides the nation state its key characteristic—temporal depth and persistence over time.

Nation

With this as a backdrop, let us now try to define what we mean by the term, nation? Steven Grosby, Professor at Clemson University, states, "*The nation is a territorial community of nativity. One is born into a nation.* The nation is one among a number of forms of kinship (e.g., family, tribe, city, state or various ethnic groups). *It differs because of the greater extent of its territory but also because of its relatively uniform culture that provides stability and a continuation—over time.*"

Nations have their own understandings of their distinctive past. This is *what separates "us" from "them" or from a hostile and threatening "non-self," the "other." This shared past is conveyed through stories, myths and history. In India we have the national epic of the Mahabharata—which tells the story of a country called Bharat and the wars that it fought over the idea of political legitimacy and political systems.* While most Indian kingdoms were monarchies, there were also Republics in that ancient era. Above all was the concept of the Chakravartin ruler who, like the Chinese Emperor, loosely ruled "all under heaven" and provided legitimacy to the notion of a nation called Bharat.

The Japanese nation state, for example, traces its descent to the myth of the worship of the Sun Goddess, Amaterasu, whose temple is at Ise. The Japanese Emperor is said to have descended from the Sun Goddess and sired the Japanese race. The historical accuracy of this myth or otherwise is not germane to the issue. What is far more germane is the tenacity and strength of the shared belief over space and time.

Zionism, the Jewish national movement, had as its goal the creation of a Jewish national state in Palestine, the ancient homeland of the Jews. Though Zionism originated in the nineteenth century, it got an impetus with the Balfour Declaration in 1919 and the unimaginable horrors that were visited upon the Jewish people in Europe during the Nazi reign which finally resulted in the creation of the state of Israel by the United Nations in 1948. This Jewish state represents a continuation of the ancient attachment of the Jews and of the Jewish religion to the historical region of Palestine.

Nations are thus formed around shared, self-designating beliefs that have such a structure. These self-designating and shared beliefs are called collective self-consciousness or a distinctive culture and tradition. This culture serves to distinguish it from all the rest.

Nations formed around these shared beliefs are not merely about a distinctive but a spatially shared past. There is a spatial focus to the relation between the individuals who constitute a nation. The idea of the nation is linked to a given geographic space or expanse of territory.

Territorial Instinct

At the basis of the nation state, howsoever anachronistic it may sound, is the animal instinct for territory. Even animals mark out their territory by scent markers of droppings and urination. All animals need a particular geographic space to live and feed/ forage and express themselves. The bigger the animal the more space it needs to express and sustain itself. This territory instinct is at the basis of the animals' "Fight-Flight" response. Near the periphery of its territorial space, an animal will flee. At its core or its centre, it will fight to its death. The animal kingdom therefore is deeply programmed genetically to think in terms of ownership of geographical space or territory. That is the basis of the territorial instinct that mankind seems to have inherited in the course of its evolutionary descent. It is a primal instinct and a very powerful one at that. It is the core of the present-day concept of nationalism and nation states.

The term nation, therefore, refers both to the land and its people. They are unified by the notion of territory and birth. The citizens of the nation and their ancestors were all born into this Homeland. The nation therefore is a social relation with both temporal depth and bounded territory.

The national consciousness is sustained by rituals, symbols (flags, emblems, anthems) and a shared history. Parents transfer to their offspring not only physical genes, but also cultural memes—the cultural inheritances from a distant past—their language, customs, religion, etc., of the larger group. Birth within its territory confers citizenship. It is recognised as the primary criterion for the membership of the nation. The nation *comingles two lines of descent—descent in the territory of the nation (the Homeland concept) and genetic descent from parents who are members of the nation.* The focus of the nation is territorial descent. Patriotism is a consequence of the preoccupation with the continuation of the self, both in its biological and cultural components. *The love that one has for the nation is designated by this term "patriotism." It is an incredibly powerful emotion for it has its roots in the deep-seated territorial instinct that can lead a person to fight to his or her death in the protection of the space identified as an extension of the self. It has led to amazing deeds of self-sacrificial altruism* as also brutal massacres. Patriotism leads one to transcend the narrow ego and identify with *the far larger cultural construct of the nation that extends not only through space but also through time.* One is now identifying the self with a far larger entity that transcends the self and changes the very mode of self-centred behaviour devoted to purely preserving the organism. This self-transcendence and identification can reach extreme levels.

Ernest Renan, the French scholar, asks in his essay "What is a nation?" and answers, "It is a coming together over time of previously distinct populations that have much in common. It implies a bounded, territorial community of customs and laws." The term nation implies a continuation over time of a relatively uniform territorial culture. A nation needs the following:

Extensive territory a

A self-designating Name

A centre (a National Capital Region) with national institutions, e.g., monuments, temples, a Parliament, a Supreme Court, a National Army, etc.

A history that asserts and expresses its temporal continuity

Relatively uniform culture—often based on a common language, religion and law

Each of these characteristics, however, is rarely found to be absolute or complete.

The Nation State

The nation now seeks to express itself through a nation state out of a dire necessity to protect and preserve the lives of its members. The nation, through its representatives and institutions, can act to secure its protection and preservation in the world. To do this, nations invent trans-individual traditions. They build monuments, mausoleums, museums and temples. They hold celebratory mass rituals, pageants and parades. The reaffirmation of traditions and its transmission from one generation to the next necessarily involves modification to the tradition. Nevertheless, there has to be a core of continuity that imparts temporal depth to the idea of the nation state. Legal developments support the establishment of a territorial relation of the nation and this must invariably include the formation of a National Army.

A nation therefore is defined as a relatively extensive territorial relation of nativity. The purpose of the state is – as a territorially extensive yet bounded social-relation for the generation, transmission and sustenance of life. *When it becomes a nation state, it is also a structure for the protection of life. The modern nation state that emerged after the Treaty of Westphalia in 1648 is characterised by a total monopolisation of violence* within its territory. It is characterised by a triangular relationship between the state, its uniformed Armed and Police Forces (that have the sole right to bear and use arms) and a wholly disarmed population. All modern nation states must thoroughly disarm their population to enforce a monopoly of violence. This is a primal condition for the coming into being of a nation state.

Britain for example has *an Armed Forces Covenant that sets out the relationship between the nation, the government and the armed forces. It recognises that the whole nation has a moral obligation to members of the armed forces and their families, and it establishes how they should expect to be treated.*

The covenant's two principles are that:

- the armed forces community should not face disadvantage compared to other citizens in the provision of public and commercial services
- *special consideration is appropriate in some cases, especially for those who have given most, such as the injured and the bereaved.*

The primary characteristic of a nation state is its complete monopoly on violence. It has to disarm all its people and retain the capability for violence solely for the members of its uniformed Armed forces and police forces who alone are permitted to bear arms—for the protection of the state and its people. Nation states like Pakistan, on the other hand, that indiscriminately weaponise their societies could unravel as a direct consequence of the negation of this vital principle of nation state formation. The problem in post colonial India was the insistence of its elite that

India as a nation had been formed by the tools of soft power. As such it had no need to monopolise violence. It did not need any armed forces! It did not believe in violence!

Thus the Nehruvian construct of nation hood flew strongly in the face of the Westphalian model of nation states that has been in vogue since 1648 (The Treaty of Westphalia). Sardar Patel prevented Nehru from disarming the new born nationstate. Tragically he died soon after India became a Republic.

Fortunately the very real threat from Pakistan and the humiliating defeat of 1962 by the Chinese forced India to rearm and expand its military forces. A nation states prime duty is to defend itself and its people. If a nation state disarms itself – it will cease to be a nation. That precisely has been the very bane of India historically. A refusal to pay attention to its military. This has led to successive defeats and enslavement. In such a scenario Gandhian Non-violence can prove to be extremely dangerous.

Homeland

Given its vast cultural diversity and heterogeneity, what suits India best is the *construct of the nation as Homeland, and by extension the Fatherland/Motherland. It is homeland or territory into which each of us is born*—whether Hindu, Muslim, Sikh, Christian, or belonging to any faith or belonging to no faith at all, is not germane to the concept of nationalism. *Birth in a territory, to parents who were born here, qualifies one for the citizenship or belonging to a Homeland. The image of the territory becomes a conceptual point of reference in the trans-individual meaning of relations within the nation. This image is not only spatially expansive but is also temporally deep.* The territorially extensive homeland of the nation is viewed as a home. It too is a structure of anxiety reducing—familiarity.

Thus a part of the self has been put into the spatial structures (the familial home or one's national homeland). These are perceived to be locational frameworks for the very generation and transmission of life. For the family, the primary focus is the parents but for the nation it is the territory. Spatial attachment to the family home can be quite pronounced, especially when a family has lived in the same home for generations and when one's parents are buried/cremated in the immediate area of the home. In the latter case, a part of oneself, those who imparted life to you, has literally been put into the inanimate land. This deeply strengthens the territorial instinct and enhances the cultural significance of the spatial territory of the nation to its citizens. Most patriotic poems and ditties cite the "ashes of the fathers and the temples of the Gods" as an object of reverence. The Japanese worship the ancestors and by extension, the land they peopled. The land is deemed an extension of the self and is life giving and sustaining. *Not only does the Homeland sustain physical life and nature, it also sustains the cultural memes and habits of nurture and ensures their transmission and continuation over time.*

Is India a Nation?

This brings us to the seminal question—is India a nation? There is a view that there was really no historical nation like India and it is only the British who forged its diverse and squabbling populations into a Nation State that emerged only in 1947.This is one of the most trenchant colonial narratives handed down to us, and even 70 years later we have not been able to grow out of this thesis and mindset. The need for foreign rule was justified on the sole basis of India being a combustible mix of so many races, reigions, ethnicities, castes, creeds and languages. The tame acceptance of foreign rule stemmed from an a priori acceptance of the deeply fractured and divided nature of the Indian polity. The British had, over two centuries, succeeded in destroying the very Idea of India itself.

In India, this remarkable continuity over time, however, spans over five millennia. Eight millenniums if we go by the latest carbon dating of Rakhig and Aarhana It has survived repeated invasions and colonial campaigns to stamp out the very idea of India. The very concerted colonial campaign to eradicate the pan-Indian identity, failed to prevent the re-emergence of the nation state in India. India, as a state, however, is *yet to recover fully from the terribly divisive strategies inflicted upon it during the two centuries long colonial era.* A large number of educated Indians still subscribe to the colonial hypothesis that India was never a nation state. They aver that only the British Empire had welded the warring castes and clans into a governable entity. This is testimony to the very successful British colonial establishments attempt to destroy the very idea of India and to reduce it to a welter of castes, creeds, tribes and linguistic communities.

This colonial construct needs to be contested strongly. The idea of the nation, actually, has deep roots in India. The Indian civilisation is the oldest living civilisation on the face of this earth. The threads of continuity can be traced back to the seals of the Indus valley civilisation that depict a proto Shiva in a Yogic posture of meditation. Surrounded by animals, he can be recognised as the Pashupatinath—the Lord of animals, or the Shiva of today, who is considered the archetypal Yogi. There are the ancient Vedas, thousands of exquisite hymns that were memorised and passed on orally from generation to generation for over a thousand years. It was the most incredible feat of the preservation of collective memories in any culture. The last of the Vedas, the Atharva Veda, clearly speaks of the *Rashtra* or nation. There are, in addition, the epics of Ramayana and Mahabharata, that still exercise a powerful hold upon the collective imagination of the Indian people. These epics describe and demarcate the geographic and cultural space of the Indian subcontinent. They have a self-designating name for this nation. It was called "Bharat," a name that has come down to us even today. Till this day, this self-designating name is used in all important Hindu rituals. *Jambu Dweepe Bharat Khande* is an incantation that situates the performer of the Hindu rituals in the world island of *Jambu Dweep* (Asia) and the territory of a nation called *Bharat.*

The problem in the Indian context is, that this civilisational and cultural unity has very rarely been transformed into political unification. In these 5000 years, the entire territory of India was unified only thrice for three episodes that roughly lasted some two centuries each. These were the unifications effected by the South Asian empires of the Mauryas, the Mughals and the British. The present Indian Republic is the successor entity of the British Empire, albeit a partitioned (trifurcated) successor. There were problems with the long interludes of break-up and disarray that came in-between the unifications of the empires. Despite this, the idea of India (Bharat) and the Indic civilisation however have been an undeniable historical fact. The temporal continuity of the idea of India is spatial as well as over long periods of time stretching into aeons. There is a stream of cultural continuity over space and time that is remarkable for its extent and duration. India is a civilisational state, even like China.

The Mahabharata talks of warriors from Assam and Nagaland (Gatokkatch is a Naga warrior and Bhagadatta is a king of Assam who is the best Elephant warrior in the whole country), as also from Afghanistan (Gandhara), Mathura, Maghada, Kuru, Panchala, Kamboj and Vanga desha (present-day Bengal) and many other provinces of present-day India. Thus Kautilya, a Brahmin scholar reputedly from South India (Kerela), was the National Security Advisor of Chandragupta Maurya, the first emperor, who founded the Mauryan Empire from Pataliputra in East India. The Adi Shankaracharya best highlighted this cultural unity in the seventh century AD, when he constructed four monasteries in the four remote corners of India (in all four cardinal directions). Interestingly, to highlight the unity of the idea of India, he appointed abbots to these monasteries from diametrically opposite areas/ regions of India. Thus an abbot from North India presided over the monastery in South India (Kanchipuram), and one from the West in the East coast monastery at Puri. Similarly, the abbot at the Badrinath Dham in the North is always chosen from South India. The Adi Shankaracharya himself came from the deep South, from the state of Kerala. These were deliberate attempts to highlight the deep cultural unity of the Indic civilisation and its remarkable continuity over space and time.

India has been a cultural melting pot, a land of synthesis. Countless races and tribes have poured from all over Asia into its fertile plains. Whatever their origins, they came to this vast homeland in wave after wave, and settled down here. India became their "Homeland" and it is the concept of this Homeland that makes India a nation, despite its bewildering diversity of languages, races, religions and tribes. The common pool of memories is spatially shared across the cultural and temporal extent of the Indian sub-continent. What defines the Indic civilisation is its wonderful assimilative ability to synthesise diverse strands into a culture of unity that still manages to preserve the diversity.

There was, however, one significant departure from this homeland tradition. The British Empire was run by a European race that refused to settle down in India permanently and become a part of this Homeland. To overcome the foreignness and exteriority of their rule, they propagated an insidious ideology that sought to destroy the very idea of India. They claimed that India had never been a nation and that its badly divided people were so much at war with one another that only a Foreign power could be impartial and objective and provide Imperial justice and fair play to its warring populations. For two centuries, the British Empire expended its tremendous energies in creating and widening major faultlines in the Indian body politik. They justified foreign rule in India on the premise that India was never a nation but a huge cauldron of disparate races, castes and ethnicities, forever at war with one another. Such a heterogeneous population was incapable of ruling itself. One or two pernicious practices in some sections of society like child marriage, sati, etc., and territorial spats between competing fiefdoms were highlighted to justify this theory that only an external power could provide imperial justice to the warring religions, castes and tribes of India. Only external rule could be impartial and objective and hence just. Thus was propagated a concept of Imperial Justice as the cornerstone of the colonial empire that was inherently extrinsic, extractive and hugely exploitative. Over a period of almost two centuries, the victims of this colonial narrative completely and thoroughly internalised this pernicious discourse of inferiority and divisiveness. India, a prosperous land of contented people and plentitude, was now plagued by famines. Its self-sufficient political economy was wilfuly destroyed by the colonisers by plunder, efficient extraction of loot and dumping of its own industrialised goods in these captive markets.

No other nation state in recent history has ever been subjected to two centuries of such a concerted cultural assault, designed to destroy its self-consciousness of itself as a nation. No other nation state has ever been subject to such a concerted assault upon the very fundamental idea of its being and had the considerable energies of an empire_expended primarily to divide and splinter its population along the faultlines of religion, caste, tribe and language. The colonial administration did everything in its power to divide and fracture the population; encourage competing groups to fight for British patronage, humiliate the natives and instil in them a deep feeling of inferiority about their own heritage and culture. The British attempt was to effectively destroy the very idea of India and make sure that after the great uprising of 1857, its diverse populations would never again unite to threaten the colonial hold of the British Empire. Despite all their efforts to prevent it, however, this is precisely what happened in the end.

There were three distinct strands in the freedom struggle of India. The Anglophile Indian elite had begun the freedom struggle in a very effete way by appealing to Imperial Justice—pleading and putting up petitions and memoranda to the Queen Empress for a measure of autonomy or home rule. They considered themselves as loyal subjects of the Empire and petitioned the queen against their local colonial rulers. Even this request for Home Rule or

Dominion status was turned down on racist grounds. India participated enthusiastically in the First World War, in the fond hope of earning British gratitude. What it got instead was the racist massacre of Jallianwala Bagh in Amritsar. This, just a year after the war, in which 1.3 million Indians had participated and some 72,000 had laid down their lives. This was a critical turning point in India's Freedom Struggle.

Mahatma Gandhi appeared on the scene at this stage and carried out a mass mobilisation of the Indian peasantry. *This was a movement of non-cooperation with the British rulers. How could they rule the people of India without their consent? He asked the people of India to boycott British goods. This mass mobilisation shook the British. Gandhi however kept it non-violent, and the British soon found non-violence to be entirely within their tolerance thresholds.* In fact, they even tacitly encouraged this strain of the freedom struggle. While practising democracy at home, they could not allow themselves to be seen as not encouraging it in their colonies.

The third strand of this struggle was the violence of the Revolutionaries like Bhagat Singh and Chandra Shekhar Azad. This worried the British and they were ruthless in its suppression. What finally led to the eclipse of the British Empire in India, however, was the violence of Netaji Subhash Chandra Bose and his Indian National Army (INA). Though it lost the battles of Imphal and Kohima, it won the War for India's Independence by instigating massive armed rebellion in the Indian Armed Forces. The military men of the INA and the regular armed forces were however rapidly marginalised, by a set of collaborators and closet Anglophiles, *as was Mahatma Gandhi.*

A benign movement led by Anglophile lawyers, most of whom had studied law in Britain, took charge in New Delhi. They modelled the Indian Constitution on the British India Act of 1935 and made social Justice the foremost principle enshrined in the Indian Constitution. It was a thinly disguised idea grafted from the concept of Imperial Justice as the cornerstone of the empire. The amazing fact however is that even after two centuries of abject racial humiliation and a most concerted attempt by the British Empire to stamp out the very idea of India—it resurfaced strongly in the Freedom Struggle, and by 1947, India was once again a free nation state. Strong nationalist leaders like Sardar Patel moved decisively to force the Indian princely states to merge with India and thus create a coherent and contiguous, territorial nation state.

Proto-Nations and Modern Nations

As highlighted earlier, *the case of India as a nation is unique. No other nation has been subjected to such a sustained cultural assault to destroy its identity. This colonial assault was all-pervasive. It used the tools of governance by way of census exercises to highlight caste differences; it created separate electorates for religious groups and then created the scheduled castes and tribes.* It also included the very system of education that was moulded to shape the attitudes of the Indian subjects as also in art and culture to highlight the so-called congenital inferiority of the Indic civilisation, and its constantly warring conglomerate of castes and creeds. Pavan K. Varma writes in "Becoming Indian: the Unfinished Revolution of Culture & Identity," *"Colonialism was such a deeply dislocating event because its critique was internalised by its victims ... In such a process, ... an entire culture attempts to reinterpret itself in terms that will somehow win the dominant outsiders' (colonisers') approval. They finally end up as caricatures, divorced from their own cultural milieu and perpetually alone—in spite of their best efforts at emulation (of their colonisers)."*

British educationists like Macaulay had ensured that the *colonisation of the Indian mind* was so thorough and complete that over seven decades after independence, the dominant colonial narrative of imperial justice and induced civilisational inferiority, still haunts the Indian narrative. Under the cloak of left-wing liberalism, the entire intellectual discourse in India is still premised around the colonial anchor of Imperial Justice. It refuses to see India as a nation state and continues to emphasise the disruptive discourse of caste and creed to divide and fragment the pan-Indian identity. This is a crass attempt to perpetuate the colonial legacy of divide and rule. Its central construct is that Indian society is deeply divided and fractured.

The British were finally forced to leave because escalating revolts in the British Indian Armed Forces made it impossible for them to continue to govern India. They left finally, but the colonial narrative that they left behind, continues to dominate in various ways the intellectual landscape in India to this day.

Nations and Proto-Nations

There is a school of thought which feels that the proto-nations of history—even historic nations like China and Japan—were not nation states in the real sense of the term. Nation states, they aver, could only come into being with the major advances in communications brought about by printed books, newspapers and periodicals and then the radio and TV mediums along with the telephone; and now the mobile, Internet and the dark-net. These communication media resulted in the creation of literate populations and thereby stabilised previously oral cultures and their languages through the print media. They also served to disseminate that language throughout the nation's territory. Thus, these new communication media promoted the national culture and consolidated territorially bounded linguistic communities. All these factors have contributed to the definition of the self in the collective conscious of the nation. It is this that leads so many scholars to conclude that nation states are a historically recent phenomenon and the proto-nations of the past were never really true nation states.

That is why most intellectuals in India are convinced that the nation state in India emerged only after 1947 and that the Proto-nations of the past formed by the Mauryan and Mughal empires (that unified the territory, enabled a common legal system, created a central army and monetised the Indian economy on the silver standard) were never really nation states in the true sense of the word. As such they fully subscribe to the colonial discourse of the empire, which maintained that India was never a nation and in fact, its population was so divided and fractured that it could never govern itself but needed to be governed by an external foreign power to ensure justice and equity to its constantly warring population segments, divided so thoroughly by caste and creed.

Pre-Modern Nations

The current narrative then is that *pre-modern nations that lacked these multiple media for national consolidation, were really not nations in the true sense of the word. Pre-Modern nations were created by myths—myths like the Sun Goddess myth of Japan and the Mahabharata of India.* These myths contributed to the formation of the image of a bounded, territorial relation of temporal duration. These formative myths, which are really beliefs with no empirical foundation, accomplish this unification by formulating connections between historically actual societies to a perceived order of the universe (through the act of Gods), e.g., formation of the Japanese nation by the Sun Goddess through the agency of the Emperor. By this process, *the historical uniqueness of the territorial community is justified. Thus, the historian Delmar Brown observes that in the process of the formation of nations, we see the device of making myths more historical and making actual events more mythical.* It is through its history—broadly understood here, to also include the formative myths, that as such blur the distinction between fact and meaningful fancy—that a nation uses to understand itself and in so doing, constitutes itself.

The culture of these pre-modern societies was fragmented both vertically and horizontally. Vertically, differences existed between the educated elite (who knew Sanskrit in the Indian context) and the illiterate peasants who were far more attached to their separate localities. Thus, ancient societies exhibited sharp cultural and political distinction between the ruling centre and the host of culturally isolated localities. This is *what impels modern scholars to question how pre-modern states could become national communities. These need the unifying agencies of the modern means of communications, public education, a uniform territory and pervasive laws and democratic citizenship.* A lot of emphasis is based on the last-named factor. In fact, the democratic concept of citizenship has contributed massively to the establishment of nation states. Democracy promotes a belief in the equality of the members of a nation, thereby contributing in a significant way to the sense of nation as a community. What then really welds a modern nation together are three critical factors:

Democratic Conception of Citizenship

Extensive market for manufactured goods and services

Advances in Communications

Without these modern prerequisites, nation state formation is impossible, aver the scholars. Hence India was never a nation state before 1947.

This view is now being challenged by a more nuanced and accurate appraisal of pre-modern societies. The spread of major world religions in antiquity like Buddhism, Christianity and later Islam calls into question the supposed cultural isolation of populations that were largely illiterate. In fact, thousands of years ago, the simple tenets of Shamanism had propagated to all continents of the world—from Asia to Africa, the Americas and Australia, in societies that were wholly illiterate. There was an amazing degree of commonality between the shamanic theory and practices in the diverse continents of the world. The magnificent spread of Buddhism across the whole of Asia by a saffron clad army of Indian monks is yet another feat of communication that would be difficult to replicate even in today's era of the Internet and satellite communications.

In fact, the spread of world religions in antiquity, indicates that extensive relations throughout vast populations and across great distances can indeed be formed even in the absence of mass-produced books, newspapers, railways and markets for industrial goods. Moreover, a study of history highlights that law codes were found throughout antiquity and the Middle ages—as well as conceptions of territories with fairly well defined boundaries.

To sum up this discussion, therefore, ancient or modern, the *following characteristics are needed for the formation of a nation state*:

A self-designating name

A written history

A degree of cultural uniformity, often as a result of and sustained by religion

Legal Codes

An authoritative centre

The conception of a bounded territory

On each of these criteria, ancient India qualifies as a nation. Its self-designating name was Bharat and later Hindustan (from the Arabic for Hindu based on Sindhu—the cradle river of the Indian civilisation). It had an extensive oral and written history in the form of the Vedas, the Puranas and the national epics of the Ramayana and the Mahabharata, which still exercise such an extensive hold upon the popular imagination. Iqbal wrote, "*Hai Ram ke wajood par Hindustan ko Naaz*" (India is proud of the legacy of Rama). The Hindu religion provides a great modicum of cultural uniformity. Beyond that (and often because of the mystical nature of Hinduism per se), we see an astonishing culture of tolerance and cross-cultural synthesis. Hinduism recognised the difference between men and outlined different paths to union with the transcendent reality, by way of Bhakti—Yoga, Gyan Yoga, Karma Yoga and Raj Yogas designed to suit very different psychological temperaments. This Vedic stanza sums up this integrative tendency, "*ekam sad, vipra bahuda vadanti*—That truth is one, the wise call him by many names." All the multifarious paths that are, ultimately lead to the same, self-transcendent reality. Hinduism, unlike sematic religions of the desert, has what Rajiv Malhotra calls "an open architecture".

Coming to the legal codes and their widespread applicability, the codes of Manu date back to the Vedas. The Arthashastra codifies the laws that governed the Mauryan Empire. The Mughals had elaborate codes for jurisprudence and the delivery of justice. The authoritative power centre in India has oscillated between Pataliputra and Delhi, and the conception of a bounded territory goes back to Jambu Dweepe-Bharat Khande—the Sanskrit incantation about territorial designation that is chanted before performing every Hindu ritual even today. Quite incidentally, the Atharva Veda talks of Rashtra or nation.

Thus India was not entirely a colonial construct. It was certainly not a gift of the British Empire. Nor was democracy a British transplant in Indian soil. There were clan republics in India in the times of Mahabharata and the Buddha. The Indian empire of the Mauryas spread the Indian ideology of Buddhism to every corner of Asia. India is a significant historical entity deeply entrenched in the collective conscious of the Indic civilisation of South Asia. It faced the challenge of Muslim invasions—largely by absorbing and synthesising the Muslim population in its melting pot. The most significant challenge, however, was now from the British Empire, which consciously sought to destroy the very idea of India and mounted the most vicious challenge by systematically fracturing its population along caste and creed faultlines. The parting gift of the empire was the partition of India by carving out the Muslim homeland of Pakistan. Pakistan today has broken up and India now has the second largest Muslim population in the whole world—ingested relatively peacefully into its fabric. The British had tried to destroy the idea of India but they failed.

Today, the idea of India has resurrected itself. Wars with China and Pakistan (the hostile other) have deepened the idea of India by projecting it against a hostile non-self—the other. The problem in

India is that petty politicians had revived the colonial project of fracturing the Indian polity again on caste and creed lines for purely personal gain. That is why the revival of right-wing nationalism in 2014 has been such a significant historical phenomenon but one that sadly seems to be losing its initial momentum.

Failure to Militarise

The legacy of the non-violent Gandhian struggle led to the coming to power of a very pacific elite who professed to abhor the use of violence. India is a country that has been invaded, looted, raped and conquered for over eight centuries. It needed to militarise and protect itself from grave external threats and internal challenges. A series of foreign invasions and attacks forced India to militarise – expand and modernise its military and for a time (in the Shastri and Indira Gandhi eras) and even with Rajiv Gandhianism was quietly given the go bye. The First NDA government of Atal Bihari Vajpayee made India a nuclear power and was quick to employ fairly massive military force in Kargil and Op Parakram. The second NDA regime of Modi was perceived as hard right. It was expected to put major emphasis upon strengthening and enhancing the role of the military in its dealings with external and internal challenges. To the nations intense surprise it has sought to revive the legacy of Mahatma Gandhi – even as it talks of Sardar Patel and his real politik. However Nuclear deterrence in South Asia, unfortunately, seems to have convinced it that, use of large scale military force is no longer possible. The use of tactical scale surgical strikes of limited violence and depths seems to be the preferred option and that too very sparingly . There is surprising emphasis being given to the Gandhian ideology of non-violence. There has been an apparent marginalisation of the military and far greater emphasis on the Police and Intelligence operations. The new found notion seems to be convinced that this is all that is needed to defend India. Large scale use of military force has apparently been ruled out. One hopes this is a temporary phase stemming from India's greatly delayed military modernisation.

What is causing concern however is a refusal to use more that token military force in J&K and the insurgents in the North East on the plea of preserving human rights. There is major emphasis on peace building through political initiatives which are inordinately stretched out and have emboldened hostile elements. Indian force usage in CI/CT operations has been confined to small arms along. This is in sharp contrast to what the USA, Russia, China, Pakistan, Myanmar and Sri Lanka have done. They have used major military force to crush armed rebellions. India has been constraining use of military force and adopting an overly pacific stance that is actually hampering peace building in the troubled state. Less Mizoram and Punjab, no other insurgency has been decisively quelled. The simple question is, a nation that has been invaded and conquered for 800 years needs to protect itself. That is the very purpose of the nation state. Gandhian ideology seriously weakens the resolve to use force to protect its citizens from external and internal threats. That is why the ideology of Bose and the INA will have to prevail over the pacific ideology of Gandhian non violence. That had, unfortunately failed to get us our freedom. Revival of this Gandhian anachronism today, could endanger the survival of the Indian Republic. We must heed the lessons of our history and devise the means to protect ourselves. Other democracies like USA and even Great Britain put very heavy emphasis on military power to protect the nation state. 70 per cent of American Presidents have been military men. The military has great influence in National Security policy formulation in the USA and UK. India's pacific culture provides a stark contrast where the Indian military is sadly marginalised. India as a nation state has to come to terms with the notions of violence and use of Force to protect the Westphalian nation state. Voluntarily disarming the state or refusing to use the force available can endanger the very survival of the state in India.

PM Modi came back with a resounding majority in the 2019 elections. Armed with this majority now in both houses of parliament, NDA 2.0 began to act with vigour and dicisiveness not seen heretofore. The most significant and bold move was the abrogation of Article 370 and bifurcation of J&K into two union territories. It was a proactive piece of legislation that clearly foresaw the turbulence that would follow an American withdrawal from Afghanistan and acted proactively to head it off. For the first time adequate force levels were deployed and succeeded in totally pacifying the valley.

12

Postscript

The Resurrection of Bose and the Indian National Army

The sum and substance of this book is that India gained its independence in 1947, almost entirely due to the catalysing impact of Bose and his Indian National Army (INA). Though the INA lost the Battles of Imphal and Kohima, it had actually won the war for India's Independence.

How?

By the widespread riots triggered by the INA trials in November-December 1945 and subsequently by the Naval Mutiny and other mutinies in the Indian Army and Air Force. Cumulatively these convinced the British that they could no longer count on the loyalty of the Indian Sepoy to the Raj. That indeed had been the centre of gravity of the colonial rule—its success at nativisation—that had enabled it to recruit an army of Indian sepoys who helped them conquer India and then rule it for over 200 years. In wartime they had expanded it to 1.3 million men in the First World War and in the Second they had raised a record all-volunteer army of 2.5 million Indians sans any conscription. The Indian soldiers had performed brilliantly well in all these wars and conflict and held the British empire together.

Bose and his INA had completely eroded this loyalty of the Indian sepoy to the Raj and this spectre of a mutiny by 2.5 million battle hardened Indian soldiers had forced them to pack their bags and leave in 1947—just two years after they won the Second World War.

The INA's ultimate triumph however turned into an unmitigated tragedy for the force itself. Bose and the INA had succeeded in driving the British out. The Raj however turned the tables entirely. It did not hand over power to the INA. In fact it used the Congress to pacify the mutinies breaking out in the Indian Armed Forces. It headed off widespread revolt by hastily handing over power to a notably anglophile dispensation in the Congress led by Pandit Nehru.

There is more to Nehru's role as a virtual collaborator of the Raj than meets the eye. The Congress Working Committee (CWC) wanted Sardar Vallabhbhai Patel as India's First Prime Minister (PM). Fourteen of the 16 members of the CWC had voted in his favour. The British prevailed upon Gandhi to anoint Nehru as the PM. Nehru's first act was to anoint Lord Louis Mountbatten as the first Governor General of Independent India.

This touching act of faith for a departing colonial administration against which a long-drawn freedom struggle had been waged is unprecedented in the annals of freedom struggles anywhere in the world. India did not become free in 1947, it became a Dominion headed by a British Governor General. So did Pakistan—but it at least chose one of its own (Jinnah) however as the first Governor General. Nehru chose Mountbatten and that is the irony. The Raj which had not batted an eyelid as 2.5 million Indians had died in the Bengal famine was bid its farewell with so much affection and bonhomie. The grateful coterie of Congressmen acted as if Freedom was a gift bestowed upon her subjects by the Queen. Had Bose taken charge the parting would have been a far more bitter and decisive break sans such bonhomie and unwarranted displays of affection.

Mountbatten's first order was to stop any INA soldiers from being taken back in the Indian Army. They were in fact treated as traitors by the new government of a supposedly free India. Their pensions were stopped. The men who fought and sacrificed so much to free India were now outright outcastes and traitors to the Empire. India became a member of the Commonwealth—collective gratitude—I suppose for the famines they had caused during the colonial era.

Unfortunately, ostracisation of the INA did not stop here. To claim political legitimacy for Nehru and his Non-Violence, the entire narrative of the freedom struggle was twisted and spin-doctored by a set of court historians. Violence of the INA, they said, had absolutely no role to play in India's freedom. It was all the creed of Ahimsa that had persuaded the British to leave. They in turn had gifted freedom to the natives and for this act of kindness Indians had to be eternally grateful to the Queen.

Since non-violence had proved so efficacious, Nehru set himself up as the high priest of Ahimsa and preached it to the whole world. Emperor Ashoka and Lord Buddha were deemed the greatest icons of India. Nehru was now projected as the third such icon of peace and non- violence who along with Mahatma Gandhi had freed India entirely by the use of soft power and persuasion. Nehru therefore did not want India to have any armed forces. In such a pacific atmosphere, it was sacrilege to talk of the INA and 26,000 of its soldiers, who had laid down their lives. These men were consigned to oblivion and abject starvation by a wretchedly ungrateful nation. The freedom that we had attained now seems fairly cosmetic in hindsight.

In August 1947 Lord Louis Mountbatten was the supreme political authority in India. He called the shots. The Chiefs of the Indian Armed Forces were British. In fact, had the war with Pakistan over J&K not started, the Indian Army (like the Navy and the Air Force) would have continued with a British Chief of Staff till perhaps the late 1960s. Nehru's faith in the British was so touching. He just did not seem to want them to go.

The British had very efficiently carried out a transfer of power that completely and irrevocably marginalised truly hostile elements like Bose and his INA. Leftist historians were drafted to craft out a brand new narrative of State for India, based upon pacifism and non-violence as the central credo. This would lend political legitimacy to Nehru. Nehru was appointed as the new global apostle of peace and non-violence. Till the late 1960s, the Intelligence Bureau continued to report loyally to the MI-5 (British Intelligence) at London about the movements of the kin of Bose. In retrospect all this seems bizarre.

India actually began to assert its freedom from the apron strings of the Empire only in the 1970s when Indira Gandhi emerged as a strong leader and leaned on the USSR for military support to break free from the clutches of empire.

The extraordinary transfer of power to a very anglophile Indian elite had actually stymied the emergence of a strong and viable nation state in India for close to a quarter century. The Westphalian nation state is premised on the sole monopoly of violence. It has to disarm its population and retain the sole monopoly of violence through its armed forces and police forces. Nehru shocked his first British Chief of Staff by flatly declaring he did not need the armed forces. The Police alone would suffice for India. Apparently he was trying to set the lead for global disarmament.

Unfortunately it was a very dangerous precedent to set for a civilisational state that had been invaded, raped, looted and burnt continuously for the last 800 years. For such a state with this long history of invasions and subjugation, talking of non-violence was dangerous in the extreme. Just one century of humiliation had compelled Mao's China to militarise. That is just what Bose wanted to do. He vanished—his INA which earned India her freedom was completely marginalised. The British ensured a Transfer of Power which would largely keep the Raj alive in all but name and cosmetic change of flag.

That has been the monumental tragedy of the Indian Republic. We have been cheated by a self-serving, anglophile set of elite who conspired with the colonial dispensation to gain power. They remained craven in their adulation of the Raj and its narratives. Brown Sahibs revived the Raj as a brown caricature of its imperial past.

It was only in the decade of the 1970s that the emergence of a strong Indian leader in the persona of Mrs. Indira Gandhi which enabled the Indian state to finally break the puppet strings of the Raj. She however was the daughter of Jawaharlal Nehru and continued with the virtual boycott and complete sidelining of the INA.

All through these long years of Congress rule some people and organisations waged a lonely and hopeless struggle to continue with the patriotic spirit and nationalist fervour of the INA and its charismatic founder—Netaji Subhash Chandra Bose. Despite the spin-doctored narratives, the Congress failed dismally to exorcise the Ghost of Bose and the tenacious hold of this icon on the Indian collective consciouness. Organisations and individuals like the Netaji Subhash Bose INA Trust led by Brig Chikara and Col KP Singhdeo struggled valiantly to keep alive Netaji's principles, values and his intense spirit of nationalism and patriotism. I had joined this organisation post retirement in 2008. One of its patrons was Mr. Ajit Doval KC, former Director, IB who would subsequently go on to become the NSA. We were joined by a whole host of other organisations including Veterans India, Rashtriya Sainik Sanstha and Bharat Patriots Foundation which began to raise the emotive issue of giving due respect and recognition to Bose and the INA for their decisive role in India's freedom struggle.

Finally the great churn and decisive break with the past came with the landslide victory of the National Democratic Alliance (NDA) in 2014 General Elections. For the first time, a non-Congress, Hindi-speaking elite took charge in New Delhi with a thumping majority. It was then that a movement began to restore the lost honour of the INA and its charismatic founder—Netaji Subhash Chandra Bose. Questions were raised about our freedom struggle and the role of Bose and the INA that had been so thoroughly obliterated.

A demand soon gathered traction for release of all classified documents pertaining to Bose and the INA. It was spearheaded by the Bose family (especially Netaji's grand-nephew—Chandra Bose who later joined the BJP) and Netaji researchers like Maj Gen Bakshi, Anuj Dhar and Chandrachud. The campaign was waged in the social media, the electronic and print media and meetings on Netaji and the INA were held in several cities. Finally the Bose family kin and the researchers were invited to the PM's residence to meet him along with the Home and Foreign Ministers (Rajnath Singh and Sushma Swaraj). I had gone for this meeting and it was rather poignant that just as we assembled on the lawns of the PM's residence there was a slight drizzle as if we had received a good omen from the heavens themselves. The PM announced there and then that all the Netaji files with the government would be declassified. These lobbying efforts bore fruit and declassification of Netaji's files finally commenced on January 23, 2016 on the occasion of Netaji's 119th Birth Anniversary with a 100 files. The second lot of 50 files, third lot of 25 files, fourth batch of 25 files and fifth batch of 25 files were released subsequently on March 29, 2016, April 29, 2016, May 27, 2016 and June 29, 2016 respectively. In all, 225 files have been put in the public domain till now. Unfortunately most of the contents of these files were already in the public domain as a result of the Shanawaz, Justice Khosla and Justice Mukherjee Commissions. So not much that was radically new emerged. There were still gaps that could only be filled if the archives held in the former Soviet Union and Great Britain were declassified. The PM did raise the issue with the Russian government but these efforts have so far been stone-walled.

Organisations like the Veterans India, Rashtriya Sainik Sanstha, INA Trust and Bharat Patriots Foundation launched a countrywide campaign to restore the lost honour of the INA and its mentor. The following demands were made:

- The Prime Minister should unfurl the National Flag from the ramparts of the Red Fort on October 21, 2018, the 75th Anniversary of the Establishment of the Azad Hind Government in Exile in Singapore. This had been recognised by 12 countries.
- Installation of Netaji's statue at Rajpath—preferably under the canopy that once housed King George V's statue near India Gate.
- The surviving INA Veterans be included in the Republic Day Parade on Rajpath. Their names be included in the National War Memorial.
- A museum dedicated to Bose and the INA be inaugurated in the Red Fort on the occasion of the 75th Anniversary of the Azad Hind Government.

Rallies were held in various cities across India by these organisations. Prominent leaders who raised their voices in support were Dr. Subramaniam Swamy and Chandra Bose. A massive campaign was launched in the social media. I personally met the Defence Ministers, Manohar Parrikar and Nirmala Sitharaman, as also the Army chief Gen Bipin Rawat. They were all very helpful and supportive but the military and civilian bureaucracies were somehow obdurate and completely resistant to a cultural change of this magnitude. It was just that this was unprecedented, it had never been done before and all bureaucracies work on precedents. Despite all the mobilisation of public opinion I felt we were getting nowhere. Finally I asked for a meeting with the NSA, Mr. Ajit Doval. I knew he was very committed to the ideals and cause of Netaji .He had been one of the patrons of the INA Trust. Even at this belated stage he swung into action and moved the lethargic bureaucracies. He had the ear of the Prime Minister and convinced him to give a final push and force this change on the deeply entrenched bureaucracies. This was indeed a major breakthrough. October 21—the 75th anniversary of the day the Azad Hind Government was established in Singapore in 1943 was coming. The INA museum that was to come up in the Red fort was not as yet ready. There were battles being waged between Prof. Kapil Kumar and the Culture Ministry Bureaucrats about the design and concept and there was no way the museum could be ready at such short notice. We would miss the great symbolism of the Hakumate Azad Hind day. I suggested to Mr. Doval that the PM could unfurl the flag and lay the foundation stone of the museum which could be inaugurated a few months later on Netaji's birthday. Mr. Doval liked the idea and moved with great energy to have it implemented forthwith. He spoke to the Prime Minister the very next day and got his approval for this ceremony.

On October 21, 2018, Prime Minister Narendra Modi unfurled the National Flag at the Red Fort. It was a historic day. Along with him was Naik Lalti Ram of the INA and Chandra Bose (nephew of Netaji). The Prime Minister also laid the foundation stone of the Netaji Bose INA Museum in the Red Fort Barracks, where the trials of the INA officers had been held. It was indeed a grand and touching ceremony and historically so very significant. America celebrates July 4—the day the Declaration of Independence had been made—as their Independence Day and not the day it was handed over/gifted to them by the British. Correctly speaking, India's Independence Day should not be celebrated on August 15 but on October 21 each year. Freedom is not begged for and given—it has to be taken by force if necessary. The National Security Advisor (NSA), Mr. Ajit Doval played a pivotal role behind the scenes in making this ceremony at the Red Fort possible. The same day Veterans India and Rashtriya Sainik Sangathana along with the Forward Block led by Mr. Saini, had organised an Azad Hind Parakram Parade on Rajpath. Four INA veterans—Naik Lalti Ram, Sepoys Baghmal, Hira Singh and Parmananda Yadav were taken out in All Terrain Vehicles (ATVs) on Rajpath. Thirty Triumph Class and Indian Thunder Chief motorcycles led this parade down Rajpath. After 70 years we had managed to get the INA veterans on Rajpath. In a grand ceremony they were later honoured on the lawns of India Gate. But this was not an official recognition. It was an honour given by the citizens.

We therefore redoubled our demands that the next Republic Day the INA veterans must be brought on Rajpath as a part of the official parade. We were astonished to find the entrenched bureaucracies still offering determined resistance. All sorts of arguments were put forth. These men had violated the oath they had taken to their British masters. So that superseded their Loyalty to their own country? Wasn't this issue settled in the INA trials itself? It was the duty of Indians to fight against an occupying colonial power. The Azad Hind Govt in exile had duly declared war against Great Britain. It was a just war. The whole country had been inflamed by the INA trials. It was the most unprecedented upsurge of nationalistic fervour ever seen in colonial India. It had shaken the empire. It was amazing. Today the bureaucracy was questioning why we were free? There were mutterings about Indian army units that had fought the INA and gotten medals and awards—how would they take it? These were Nehruvian era mental blocks and reservations. The British senior officers and Lord Mountbatten had injected these reservations against the INA. One was dazed to see how deeply entrenched these reservations had become. What was amazing was that 70 years after independence the bureaucracy had so deeply internalised the colonial era mindset and hangover of the Raj. The PM was inaugurating the INA museum in Red Fort. He was to also unfurl the flag in the Andamans where the Japanese had handed over the islands to the INA ceremonially in December 2018. Wasn't that enough?

As the months went by I realised that this INA participation in the Republic Day was not likely to happen. I had again spoken to the Army Chief. The Army was still awaiting instructions from the ministry as this was a political decision that would have to come from above. The Army Day Parade was already over and still the issue was pending. At this belated stage I had no option but to seek a meeting with the NSA. He felt it was now too late. I told him it indeed was. We just had a handful of INA veterans still left alive. Those INA veterans who had come to the Red Fort were ranging in age from 110 to 97.They may not be there the next year. We could at least honour them while they were alive. Mr. Doval nodded grimly. There and then he picked up the phone and spoke to the Defence Secretary and gave executive instructions. In view of the very little time left he asked me to liaise personally with the Ministry and Army HQ and get this done. I spoke to the relatives of the INA veterans. They were delighted but after all these years they did not have their uniforms. Overnight we got them stitched. Meanwhile the MoD issued written instructions and it is to the entire credit of the officers of the Adjutant Generals Ceremonial & Welfare Branch that on just some 4 days' notice they got it all organised so very smoothly.

January 26, 2019—the 70th Republic Day of the country—four INA veterans were taken in shining Military Gypsy vehicles down Rajpath. My eyes brimmed over with tears as I saw them that day. A number of TV channels had called me to give commentary on the parade. My voice quavered with emotion and my eyes brimmed over as I saw the INA veterans go down Rajpath in those sleek Gypsies to thunderous applause from their countrymen. At long last, symbolically at least, the honour of the INA was restored. The nation had honoured them after 75 years almost. It was better late than never. My apprehension was fully justified. Just five days after the parade, Sepoy Baghmal of the INA who was 99 years old, passed away. It was as if he was only waiting for this final vindication of his and his valiant army's honour. Out of 60,000 INA men, some 26,000 had laid down their lives fighting for their country's freedom. At the behest of the last British Governor General Lord Mountbatten, they had been treated as traitors and denied their pensions. A forgotten army was honoured seven decades later by a grateful nation. It was divine and poetic justice.

Appendix

THE BRITISH COMMAND AND CONTROL STRUCTURE LONDON AND INDIA (1945-1947)

INDIA OFFICE: LONDON

Secretary of State: Lord Pethick-Lawrence (cr. Baron 16 August 1945)

Permanent Under-Secretary:Sir David Monteath

Parliamentary Under-Secretary: Mr Arthur Henderson

Deputy Under-Secretaries: Sir William Croft (from 2 January 1946 on his return from the Treasury)

Assistant Under-Secretaries: Mr P.J. Patrick

Mr G. J. Baxter

Private Secretary to Secretary of State: Mr F. F. Turnbull (until 13 February 1946 when appointed Secretary to the Cabinet Mission) Mr M. J. Clauson (from 14 February 1946)

INDIA

Viceroy, Governor-General and
Crown Representative: Field Marshal Viscount Wavell (Sir John Colville acted from 25 August15

September 1945 during Lond Wavell's absence in London)

Private Secretary to the Viceroy: Sir Evan Jenkins Mr G. E. B. Abell (from 16 November 1945)

Reforms Commissioner: Mr V. P. Menon.

EXECUTIVE COUNCIL

Commander-in Chief: General Sir Claude Auchinleck

Home: Sir Francis Mudie, I.C.S. Sir John Thorne, I.C.S. (from 15 October 1945)

Finance: Sir Archibald Rowlands

War Transport: Sir Edward Benthall (Sir Arthur Griffin acting 9 August-9 October 1945)

Posts and Air: Sir Mahomed Usman

Education, Health and Lands: Sir Jogendra Singh

Commerce, and Industries and Civil Supplies: Sir M. Azizul Haque

Food: Sir J. P. Srivastava

Labour: Dr B. R. Ambedkar

Law: Sir Asoka Kumar Roy

Commonwealth Relations: Dr N. B. Khare

Information and Broadcasting:
Sir Sultan Ahmed (until 31 October 1945) Sir

Akbar Hydari, I.C.S. (acting from 31 October 1945)

Supply: Sir Ramaswami
Defence: Mudaliar (Mr A. A. Waugh, I.C.S. acting From 17 November 1945) Sir Firoz Khan Noon (until 15 September 1945 after which portfolio was held in abeyance)

Planning and Development: Sir Ardeshir Dalal (until 28 January 1946; Sir Akbar Hydari acting thereafter)

GOVERNORS OF PROVINCES

Madras: The Hon. Sir Arthur Hope (Sir Henry Knight, I.C.S. acting from 26 February 1946)

Bombay: Sir John Colville (Sir C.H. Bristow, I.C.S. acting 25 August-14 September 1945)

Bengal: Captain Rt. Hon. R. G. Casey (Sir Henry Twynam, I.C.S. acting 13 Sep tember-11 October 1945) Sir Frederick Burrows (from 19 February 1946)

United Provinces: Sir Maurice Hallett, I.C.S. Sir Francis Wylie, I.C.S. (from 7 December 1945)

Punjab: Sir Bertrand Glancy, I.C.S

Central Provinces and Berar: Sir Henry Twynam, I.C.S. (Mr F. C. Bourne, I.C.S. acting until 11 October 1945)

Assam: Sir Andrew Clow, I.C.S.

Bihar: Sir Thomas Ruther ford, I.C.S.

North-West Frontier Province: Sir George Cunningham, I.C.S., Sir Olaf Caroe, I.C.S. (from 3 March 1946)

Orissa: Sir Hawthorne Lewis.

Sind: Sir Hugh Dow

Sir Francis Mudie (from 15 January 1946)

PRIME MINISTERS OF PROVINCES

Punjab: Malik Khizar Hyat

Khan Tiwana

Assam: Sir Muhammad Sa'adulla

Mr Gopinath Bardoloi (from 11 February 1946)

North-West Frontier Province: Dr Khan Sahib Sind
Sir Ghulam Hussain
Hidayatullah

The remaining Provinces were administered by their Governors under Section 93 of the Government of India Act 1935

PRINCIPAL HOLDERS OF OFFICE

UNITED KINGDOM CABINET

Announced 28 July and 4 August 1945 (Members of the India and Burma Committee are italicised)

Prime Minister and First Lord of
the Treasury, Minister of Defence: Mr Clement Attlee

Lord President of the Council and Leader of the House of Commons: Mr Herbert Morrison

Secretary of State for Foreign Affairs: Mr Ernest Bevin

Lord Privy Seal: Mr Arthur Greenwood.

Chancellor of the Exchequer: Mr Hugh Dalton

President of the Board of Trade: Sir Stafford Cripps

Lord Chancellor: Lord Jowitt

First Lord of the Admiralty: Mr A. V. Alexander

Secretary of State for the Home: Mr James Chuter Department

Secretary of State for India and for Burma: Lord Pethick-Lawrence (cr. Baron by Letters Patent dated 16
August 1945)

Secretary of State for the Colonies: Mr G. H. Hall

Secretary of State for War: Mr J. J. Lawson

Secretary of State for Air: Viscount Stansgate

Secretary of State for Scotland: Mr J. Westwood

Minister of Fuel and Power: Mr E. Shinwell

Minister of Education: Miss Ellen Wilkinson

Minister of Health: Mr Aneurin Bevan

Minister of Agriculture and Fisheries: Mr T. Williams

OTHER MINISTERS MENTIONED IN THIS VOLUME

Minister of Food: Sir Ben Smith

Postmaster-General: Earl of Listowel

Bibliography

Archives

"Transfer of Power," Vol. 6, Her Majesty's Stationery Office. London, 1971.

Fd Mshl Auchinleck's Reports to Viceroy, Appreciation of the Situation December 1945 and correspondence with Chief of Imperial General Staff. "Transfer of Power," Vol. 6, pp. 530, 939, 638, 673, 675, 975. (Refers to Chapter 5 of this book)

Viceroy Viscount Fd Mshl Wavells Report to HM the King, Prime Minister Attlee, Lord Pethick-Lawrence, etc. "Transfer of Power," Vol. 6, pp. 713, 1054. (See Chapter 6)

Wavell's Papers, Private Correspondence: HM the King pp. 100-2. (See Chapter 6)

Governors of Various Provinces: Report to Viceroy Fd Mshl Wavell on RIN Mutiny. "Transfer of Power," Vol. 6, pp. 542, 546, 631, 724, 807, 1071, 1079. (See Chapter 7)

Director Intelligence Bureau, Report on INA trials. "Transfer of Power," Vol. 6, p. 512. (See Chapter 8)

The Collected Works of Mahatma Gandhi, Vol. 77. The Publications Division, Government of India, New Delhi, 1979. Statements of Mahatma Gandhi to the press on release from jail, July 1944, Pp. 247, 276, 338, 417, 433 (See Chapter 3)

The Collected Works of Mahatma Gandhi, Vol. 78. The Publications Division, Government of India, New Delhi, 1979, p. 9. (See Chapter 3)

Books

1. Allen, Louis. *Burma: The Longest War 1941-1945.* St. Martins Publ., New York, 1984.
2. Ibid., *Sittang: The Last Battle.* TBS The Book Service Ltd., UK, April 2, 1973.
3. Ayer, S. A. *Unto Him a Witness: the Story of Netaji Subhas Chandra Bose in East Asia.* Thacker Publishers, Bombay, 1951.
4. Barker, A. J. *The March on Delhi.* Faber and Faber, London, UK, 1963.
5. Batliwal, S. S. and V. K. Jhaveri. *Jai Hind: The Diary of a Rebel Daughter of India with the Rani Jhansi Regiment.* Janmabhoomi Prakashan Mandir, Bombay, 1945.
6. Bose, Mihir. *The Last Hero: A Biography of Subhash Bose.* Quartet Books, London, 1982.
7. Bose, Subhash Chandra. *An Indian Pilgrim: An Unfinished Autobiography and Collected Lectures 1897-1921.* Calcutta, 1965.
8. Bose, Subhash Chandra. *Impressions in Life.* Lahore, 1947.

9. Bose, Subhash Chandra. *The Indian Struggle: 1920-34*. Lahore, 1935.
10. Caffrey, Kale, *Out in the Mandalay Sun: Singapore 1941-45*. London, 1974.
11. Chatterjee, A. C. *India's Struggle for Freedom*. Chuckervertty Chatterjee & Co., Calcutta, India, 1947.
12. Cohen, Stephen P. *The Indian Army: Its Contribution to the Development of a Nation*. University of California Press, Berkeley, Los Angeles, USA.
13. *The Constituent Assembly Debates 1946-1949.*
14. Corr, Gerard H. *The War of the Springing Tiger*. Jaico Publishing House, Delhi, 1975.
15. Crosby, Steven. *"Nationalism: A Very Short Introduction*. Oxford University Press, New Delhi, 2005.
16. Das, Sitanshu. *Subhash Chandra Bose: A Political Biography*. Rupa Publications, New Delhi, 2006.
17. De Kalyan Kumar "Netaji Subhash : The Liberator of the Indian Subcontinent". Bengal Lokmat Printers Pvt Ltd, Kolkata, 2015.
18. Dhar, Anuj. *Back from the Dead: Inside the Subhash Bose Mystery*. Manas Publications, Delhi, 2007.
19. Dhar, Anuj. *India's Biggest Cover Up*. Vitasta Publishers, New Delhi, 2012.
20. Evans, Sir Geoffrey and James Anthony Brett. *Imphal: A Flower on Lofty Heights*. London, 1962.
21. Fay, Peter Ward. *The Forgotten Army: India's Armed Struggle for Independence 1942-1945*. The University of Michigan Press; Reprint edition, October 31, 1995.
22. Ganpuley, N. G. *Netaji in Germany: A Little Known Chapter*. Bombay, 1959.
23. Ghosh, Kalyan Kumar. *The Indian National Army*. Meenakshi Prakashan, Meerut, 1969.
24. Giani, Kesar Singh. *Indian Independence Movement in East Asia*. Anarkali Publishers: Singh Brothers; 1st[s] edition, Lahore, 1947.
25. Goebbels, Joseph, translated by Lochner P. Louis. *The Goebbels Diaries, 1942-1943*. Reprinted by Greenwood Press Group, Westport, Connecticut, USA, 1970.
26. Gordon, Leonard A. *"Brothers against the Raj: A Biography of Indian Nationalists Sarat & Subhash Chandra Bose*. Viking Penguin, New Delhi, 1990.
27. Gordon, Leonard A. *The Nationalist Movement 1823-1940*. Columbia University Press, New York, 1974.
28. Griffiths, Sir Percival Joseph. *The British in India*. Robert Hale Publishers, London, 1946.
29. *INA Heroes: Autobiographies of Maj Gen Shahnawaz Khan, Col. Prem K. Sehgal and Col. Gurbax Singh Dhillon of the Azad Hind Fauj*. Hero Publications, Lahore, 1946.
30. Isemonger, F. C. and J. Slattery. *An Account of the Ghadr Conspiracy*. Lahore, 1921.
31. Iwaichi, Lt Gen Fujiwara, Yoji Akashi (translated). *F. Kikan: Japanese Army*

Intelligence Operations in Southeast Asia during World War II. Heinemann Asia Publishers, Hong Kong, May 1983.

32. James, D. H. *The Rise and Fall of the Japanese Empire.* London, 1951.
33. Khan, Maj Gen Shah Nawaz. *My Memories of the INA & its Netaji.* Rajkamal Publications, Delhi, 1946.
34. *The INA Heroes: Autobiographies of Maj Gen Shahnawaz Khan, Col. Prem K. Sehgal and Col. Gurbax Singh Dhillon of the Azad Hind Fauj.* Hero Publications, Lahore, 1946.
35. Khosla, Justice G. D. *Inquiry into the Death of Subhash Chandra Bose.* Khosla Commission 1970, Govt. of India, 1970.
36. Kiani, Maj Gen Mohammad Zaman. Edited by Sisir Kumar Bose. *India's Freedom Struggle and the Great INA.* Reliance Publishing House, New Delhi, 1994.
37. Kirby, Maj Gen S. Woodburn, Capt C. T. Addis, Col G. T. Wards, Brig M. R. Roberts, N. L. Desoer. *The War Against Japan Vol III: The Decisive Battles.* London, 1961.
38. Kirby, Maj Gen S. Woodburn et al. *The War Against Japan: The Reconquest of Burma,* Vol. IV. London, 1965.
39. Kulkarni, V. S. and K. S. N. Murty. *First Indian National Army Trial.* Mangal Sahitya Prakashan, Pune, 1946.
40. Lebra, Joyce Chapman. *Japanese Trained Armies in South East Asia.* Columbia University Press, New York, 1977.
41. Lebra, Joyce Chapman. *Jungle Alliance: Japan and the Indian National Army.* Asia Pacific Press, Singapore, 1971.
42. Madan, Gopal. *Netaji Subhash Chandra Bose: The Last Phase (in his own words),* Har-Anand Publications, New Delhi, 1994.
43. Majumdar. R. C. *History of the Freedom Movement in India - 3 vols.* Firma KLM Pvt. Ltd., Calcutta, January 1, 2004.
44. Montagu, Edwin Samuel. *An Indian Diary.* William Heinemann Publ., Germany, 1930.
45. Mukherjee, Mithi. *India in the Shadow of Empire: A Legal & Political History, 1914-1950.* Oxford University Press, New Delhi, 2010.
46. Nag, Kingshuk. *Netaji: Living Dangerously.* Authors Upfront Publishing Services, PL, November 16, 2015.
47. Ohsawa, Georges. *The Two Great Indians in Japan: Sri Rash Behari Bose and Subhash Chandra Bose.* Kusa Publications, Calcutta, 1954.
48. Palta, Krishan Raj. *My Adventures with the INA.* Lion Press, Lahore, 1946.
49. Percival, Lt Gen Arthur E. *The War in Malaya.* Orient Longmans Publ., London, 1949.
50. Prasad. Amba. *The Indian Revolt of 1942.* Delhi, 1958.
51. Ram, Moti. *Two Historic Trials in Red Fort.* Roxy Printing Press, New Delhi, 1946.

52. Safrani, Abid Hasan. *The Men from Imphal.* Netaji Oration, Netaji Research Bureau, Calcutta, 1971.
53. Singh, Maj Gen Mohan. *Soldiers' Contribution to Indian Independence.* Army Educational Stores, New Delhi, 1974.
54. Singh, Randhir. *The Ghodan Heroes.* Lahore, 1921.
55. Sivaram, M. *The Road to Delhi.* Tuttle Publishing, North Clarendon, VT, USA, June 15, 1967.
56. Slim, Field Marshall Viscount. *Defeat into Victory.* Cassell Publishers, London, 1956.
57. Swinson, Arthur. *Four Samurai: A Quartet of Japanese Army Commanders in the Second World War.* Hutchinson, London, 1968.
58. The Govt. of India. *Netaji Enquiry Commission Report.* Govt. of India, 1956.
59. Thivy, John Aloysius. *A Short Sketch of the Indian Independence Movement in Southeast Asia.* Netaji Research Bureau, Calcutta.
60. Thivy, John Aloysius. *The Struggle in East Asia.* Netaji Research Bureau, Calcutta, 1971.
61. Toye, Hugh. *The Springing Tiger.* Cassell Publishers, London, 1959.
62. Toye, Hugh. *Subhash Chandra Bose: The Springing Tiger.* Jaico Publishing House Reprint, Delhi, 2015.
63. Hayashida, Tatsuo. *Netaji Subhash Chandra Bose.* Allied Publishers, 1970.
64. Tsuji, Col Masanobu. *Singapore: The Japanese Version.* St. Martin's Press, Sydney, 1960.
65. Tuker, Lt Gen Sir Francis. *While Memory Serves: The Story of the Last Two Years of British Rule in India.* London, 1956.
66. Yadav, Capt S. S. INA. *Forgotten Warriors of Indian War of Independence (1941-46).* Indian National Army, vol. 1. Published by All India INA Committee, Delhi, 2005.
67. Nehru, Jawahar Lal. *An Autobiography.* Penguin India, new ed., 2004.
68. Nehru, Jawahar Lal. *The Discovery of India,* Penguin India, new ed., 2008.

Articles and Papers

69. Bohra, Ranjan. "Subhash Bose, the INA and the War of Indian Liberation," *Journal of Historical Review* (Vol. No. 3, 1982).
70. Bose, Dr. Sisir K. "The Great Escape," *The Illustrated weekly of India,* April 14, 1974.
71. Griffiths, Sir Percival Joseph. "The British in India," Robert Hale Publ., London, 1946.
72. Malhotra, Iqbal. "Stalin's Prisoner," *Open Magazine,* December 2016.
73. Mondal, B. "The INA's Valiant Battle in The Arakans," *Caravan,* October 1, 1973.
74. *Young India,* Weekly Paper published by the Indian Independence League, 1943-45.

Resurrection of the INA.
Four INA veterans aged 109, 108, 99 and 98 respectively on Rajpath for Republic day parade 2019. A poignant vindication of honour.

Author with Nk Lalti Ram of INA for the 75th anniversary celebration of the Formation of Azad Hind Govt in Exile.

Prime Minister Modi with Nk Lalti Ram of INA at the Red Fort for the 75th anniversary of the establishment of the Azad Hind Govt in Exile in Singapore on 21 Oct 2019.